RESPONSIBLE LIVING
IN AN AGE
OF EXCUSES

RESPONSIBLE LIVING

IN AN AGE OF EXCUSES

KURT D. BRUNER

MOODY PRESS
CHICAGO

All Scripture quotations, unless noted otherwise, are from the *Holy Bible: New International Version*. Copyright © 1973, 1978, 1984, International Bible Society. Used by permission of Zondervan Bible Publishers. All rights reserved.

ISBN: 0-8024-9097-2

3 5 7 9 10 8 6 4 2

Printed in the United States of America

*To my wife, Olivia,
my best friend and most enthusiastic cheerleader.
Without your encouragement and support,
writing would still be only a dream.*

Contents

Foreword

Just picture the scene. You're at the airport in New York with your family after a week of vacation, waiting to fly home to California. After an exhausting week of walking, shopping, and seeing the shows, you're about to board the plane when . . . it happens. A "Flight Delayed" sign goes up announcing that your plane won't be leaving on time.

As you look around, you see that it's not just your plane, but the entire airport is being shut down! For seven agonizing hours you're stuck with thousands of others who are frustrated and tired, struggling to keep your kids from tearing down the walls and unable to do anything about your predicament.

Just a frequent flyer's nightmare? Certainly not. On Tuesday, September 17, 1991, a power shortage at an AT&T switching center crashed their computer system. That left more than 1 million residents without telephone service for more than seven hours. And as an afterthought, it also shut down all of New York's major airports, delaying thousands in the New York area and affecting tens of thousands across the country who waited for connecting flights that were canceled or delayed.

What played a major role in the switching center losing power? A broken part? Faulting wiring? Try "negligence." AT&T admitted the next day that the men who manned the switching station *ignored both audio and visual alarms* that the computer system was losing power and about to crash.

It seems inconceivable that grown men would ignore flashing lights and warning bells, doesn't it? Yet Gary Smalley and I here at Today's Family consistently see the same thing happening with many men and women when it comes to their personal and family relationships.

Every week, we see people in our counseling office who have ignored warning signs for years as they've drifted closer and closer to the brink of family disaster. And unfortunately, they've tried to reverse their direction only when they've come too near the edge. That's one reason I believe that *Responsible Living* carries such an important message for men and women today.

Kurt Bruner issues a wake-up call that we need to take a close look at where we're headed in life. Are we more concerned about being liked by others than doing what is right? Have we ignored a problem for years, thinking something will change and found that it doesn't? Do we struggle with habits that have started to control us or with attitudes that have crossed the line?

In a clear and challenging way, Kurt encourages us to face our problems and even more—to reach our potential—through taking full responsibility for our attitudes and actions. Through vivid stories he shows us that we *can* succeed.

As Director of Correspondence and Research for Focus on the Family, Kurt Bruner has his finger on the pulse of what's right and wrong in the American family. I know Kurt and have seen firsthand the incredible team of "people helpers" he trains and oversees at Focus. His counsel is biblical and wise, and his stories will touch and encourage your heart.

Do you teach, counsel, or live with someone who needs to make positive personal changes? Are you ready to move upstream to greater fulfillment, effectiveness, and intimacy yourself? Then I encourage you to dig into this book and see how the insights Kurt has learned from years of helping others can help you in all your relationships today.

JOHN TRENT, PH.D.
Vice President, Today's Family

Preface

When does our need to identify the sources of life's difficulties develop into an excuse for irresponsibility? It is this question that motivated the book you hold in your hands.

Our culture has undergone a disturbing shift away from individual responsibility. We have gradually become a society full of what *Time* magazine labeled "finger pointers," "crybabies," and "eternal victims." As a result, personal initiative for advancement has been replaced with bellyaching and blame-shifting.

Much good has come from the recovery movement and its increased attention to the legitimate difficulties of life. Child abuse, racial prejudice, religious excesses, financial difficulties, and a thousand other sources of resistance confront all who live in this world. It is important that we recognize the pain of life if we hope to recover from its scars and overcome its obstacles.

Unfortunately, many have become so consumed with the process of recognition that recovery never occurs. Rather than discovering their source of difficulty in order to deal with it, they use it as an excuse for stagnation. Seeing themselves as helpless victims, they absolve themselves of personal responsibility.

On the other end of the spectrum are those who minimize the very real resistance created by life's hardships. You can almost feel a long, bony finger prodding your chest as they boast of the rough and rugged efforts they've made to overcome obstacles. Unfortunately, deep hurts have been repressed, relationships have been damaged, and compassion has been lost in the wake of their "success."

There must be a balance. We cannot ignore the hurts of life, but neither can we use them to excuse irresponsible attitudes and choices. I hope the pages that follow will prompt each person reading them to begin the journey of finding balance on a personal level.

An additional note: In order to enhance understanding and respect confidentiality, names and details have been changed on most of the personal illustrations throughout this book. Some are compilations of several representative situations; others are actual case examples. All of them touch upon threads of experience common to the human family in general and to the evangelical community in particular.

Acknowledgments

No one writes a book in isolation. The direct and indirect contributions of others have helped to formulate, sharpen, and articulate the ideas I've attempted to present. Although it would be impossible to mention each person who has played a part in the development of this book, I would like to specifically thank the following.

For providing insightful observations on the principles I've addressed: Douglas Geivett, Mary Loa, Joann Letherer, Randy Piersma, and Cathy Norman.

For their encouragement and direction in the process of writing: Rolf Zettersten, Joann Letherer, and Jim Bell.

For contributing to my life and growth in ways they will never know but without which I may not have accomplished this endeavor: Dan Allen, J. Otis Ledbetter, Diane Passno, Carol Larsen, Linda Luck, the faculty of Talbot Seminary, and my parents, who modeled and reinforced many of these principles from my earliest days.

Introduction

If life were easy, this book would not need to be written. But it isn't. From the first moments outside the warm, protective environment of our mother's womb we are hit with the stark reality that life is something less than comfortable. And as we age the harshness of living becomes more and more severe. We set out on this journey with high ideals but few skills and little understanding of how to overcome the obstacles before us. Some confront and conquer these obstacles. Others leave them unchallenged. What makes the difference?

That question became very important to me recently when my wife and I brought our first child home from the hospital. With the miracle of birth as the backdrop to the overwhelming challenge of parenthood before us, we brought Joshua Kyle into our home with excitement and joy. But coupled with our sense of gratitude for his safe arrival came the awesome realization that we would be the primary molders of his life. He would learn his first words in our living room, take his first steps into our arms, and form his early view of God by observing our walk and listening to our talk.

As his father, I have the unique opportunity to teach him what it means to do an honest day's work, catch a ball, and be a man. Yet, I also have the responsibility to instill in my son the values I cherish and the truths I have learned. Looking back on my own upbringing, I know that living a consistent life is the primary vehicle by which to do that. My father said little but spoke great volumes with his actions. Now it is I who must model manhood and character for my own child.

But I know all too well that life will be difficult for him. We will try to protect him as much as possible, but it would be futile to do so forever, not to mention foolish. Sooner or later, he must learn to confront challenges. As much as I hate the thought, he may even find himself facing tragedy. Unless he is equipped for it, he will become a defeated person.

I have a privileged opportunity to serve as Director of Correspondence and Research for Focus on the Family. Over the years, I have personally read and responded to more than twenty thousand letters from members of the evangelical community seeking advice or assistance. People openly share their secret hurts and struggles in these letters. Many of them reveal things to us that they have kept hidden from their family, friends, church, and pastor. Reading the situations of thousands of people has provided an opportunity to catch a bird's-eye view of where the various paths of life lead. I now seek to keep my son, as well as myself, from heading down those paths that lead toward failure and painful consequences.

Some Christians naively assume that we are exempt from the serious difficulties of life. After all, don't we have a divine inheritance of protection from calamity? As one who has interacted with thousands of individuals from all spectrums of the evangelical community, I can guarantee that we do not. In fact, there is little to no difference in the rate of adversity between Bible-believing Christians and the general population. We all live in a fallen world.

I have chosen to describe the harsh realities of life using the analogy of a river. Despite our strong desire to head upstream toward a healthy, balanced, and successful life, strong currents, if left unchallenged, will carry us downstream. We can choose either to be a passive victim of the current, or we can start actively paddling against it. To move upstream, however, we must have two things.

First, we need to understand and acknowledge the severity of the current. Each individual faces a different combination of circumstances and struggles that hinder his or her advancement. Some experience relatively minor resistance, whereas others feel as if life is pushing them into the white water rapids. It is important that we honestly confront the factors that contribute to the current, such as past experiences, present circumstances, the people in our lives, and even our own human tendencies.

Second, we need a paddle with which to row ourselves up-stream against the current. This paddle is an understanding of and commitment to a responsible lifestyle. Though the pull will always be strong, having the paddle will provide the means to resist it. With it, we can confidently face the obstacles before us, knowing that we have the tool for living a balanced life, maintaining healthy relationships, and attaining personal goals.

Christians often allow their hope of eternity to overshadow their sense of responsibility in this life. Though the Scriptures do contain exciting promises for the future, they also outline a plan for living in the here and now. It is that plan for living that we often fail to understand. We subvert our own advancement due to our profound misunderstanding of the biblical perspective on the responsible lifestyle. As a result, we abdicate our duty as the people of God to glorify Him in this life.

The Bible has not left us without direction, however. On the contrary, it outlines a plan for living successful and fulfilled lives, while having a positive influence on the world around us. By individually and corporately using the paddle of responsible living to actively go against the flow, we will find that this life, though not easy, can be extremely rewarding!

Section One

THE PULL OF THE CURRENT

*On the river of life are strong currents which,
left unchallenged, carry us downstream.
We can either choose to be their passive victim,
or we can start actively going against the flow.*

1
Downstream Drift

He jests at scars who never felt a wound.
William Shakespeare

There was a time when I viewed the church as a group of smiling individuals living pearly white lives in the midst of sinful society. They had managed to avoid contamination by the harmful influences of the fallen world. I was shocked when I heard about tragedy due to sin in a church family, but I regarded such events as isolated incidences, which did not color my overall picture of a people who lived generally pure and positive lives.

My optimism created a tendency in me to downplay people's legitimate struggles. *After all,* I thought, *if they would just stop wallowing in their problems and shape up, things would be as they are "supposed" to be.*

Experience has since changed my outlook. Handling correspondence for a major evangelical ministry has permanently altered my perspective. Now, rather than being shocked by scandal and tragedy, I have learned to expect it.

All people, even Christians, have problems. And problems produce a current of resistance against advancement in life. If we downplay the strength of that current or ignore it altogether we hinder our ability to resist the downstream drift. If we recognize its reality we will be able to start paddling against the flow.

The current of life can be broken down into several broad categories. First, past experiences can create a nagging pain of unbearable memories. Second, present circumstances can produce an immediate resistance to goals and dreams. Third, the people in our lives, including those we love, can hinder our advancement. Finally, and perhaps most important, our own tendencies as fallen human beings toward self-subversion carry us downstream.

PAST EXPERIENCES

Evangelicals tend to concentrate so heavily on biblical exposition that we sometimes fail to recognize the painful struggles many people face as a result of traumatic childhood experiences. Pastors can inadvertently communicate the idea that if you apply points one and two of their most recent sermon, you will overcome the unresolved issues in your life. Consequently, those in real pain try a quick fix, but it fixes nothing.

OUTSIDER

For as long as she can remember, Janice has struggled with lack of identity and poor self-image. She is painfully shy, afraid to interact with others, especially "beautiful people" who seem so sure of themselves. Others tell her she has nothing to fear and that she should just be herself. What they don't seem to understand is that "being herself" is one of the most difficult things for her to do.

As a child, Janice said little. In fact, she was so quiet that people thought she was mentally retarded. Her parents, embarrassed by her apparent slowness, gave her little emotional support. The kids at school said she was dumb and made clear that she was an unwelcome outsider. Teachers expected little from her and gave less attention to her than to other kids.

As an adult, Janice struggles with depression and has tried several different medications to combat her feelings of worthlessness. Nothing seems to help. Her shyness prevents her from talking to others, which adds to her feelings of isolation. Depression and related anger prompt her to yell and scream at those she loves, but then she feels guilty.

Janice, like many others, battles identity and self-worth problems as an adult largely due to events that took place more than twenty-five years earlier. Emotional stress, verbal abuse, and possibly even physical abuse were the realities of her childhood. Today she asks for prayer, hoping the Lord will *take away* her depression and give her the strength to overcome her shyness. Unfortunately, she has been indirectly encouraged to look for a quick fix by a "just give it to the Lord" mentality. Although it is true that the Lord has promised to go through the valley with us, Janice herself must honestly deal with her painful past in order to start resisting the current of her life.

FAMILY SECRET

Maria has difficulty trusting others, including God. When she was growing up, her family was deeply involved in their church and was regarded as the "ideal" Christian family. In a congregation that tended toward emotional and deeply felt worship, "Praise the Lord!" was a common expression. Unfortunately, the rich, deep worship was countered by poor, shallow biblical teaching. Her family had a ritual of surface religion rather than a sincere relationship.

Maria's family lived with a secret. Maria and her sisters were sexually abused by their father, the deacon. Week after week they would don their Sunday best and sit side-by-side in the pew, listening to God's anointed declare the virtues of righteous living. Then at night they would receive visits from their father.

As is typical in such situations, Maria's mother did nothing when told of the abuse. She was more concerned about how such "stories" would impact her husband's position and respect in the church than whether or not they were true. While "God's anointed" lavished praise upon the father for his apparent commitment to the Lord and sacrificial service, Maria cried out to God for help.

Although Maria has not abandoned her Christian beliefs, is it any wonder that she has difficulty grasping the truth of God's goodness and love? She wants to have a sincere relationship with God based upon truth, but the lie of her family secret is holding her back. "Praise the Lord!" still rings hollow.

Statistics regarding the occurrence of sexual, physical, and emotional abuse in children are staggering. In fact, a large percentage of the Christian community experienced abuse in one form or another while growing up. I can't count the number of letters I have read that indicate that verbal abuse, physical abuse, and even sexual molestation were part of an individual's upbringing in a "Christian" home. Though disturbing, that is a reality that must be faced.

It is impossible to deny that people like Janice and Maria have legitimate cause to struggle. The current of past experiences causes real and painful resistance to advancement. Before either of them can expect to head upstream, they must acknowledge the obstacle of past experiences.

PRESENT CIRCUMSTANCES

Hard as we may try, it is difficult to keep from letting our circumstances interfere with our objectives in life, especially when those circumstances create turmoil. Unexpected events can suddenly throw us off track, leaving us dazed and wondering what went wrong.

FREAK ACCIDENT

While playing football with the boys one weekend Gary Randall experienced a freak accident that impaired his ability to perform his job at the plant. Despite his nearly ten years with the company as a faithful employee, management could not reassign Gary to less rigorous work due to his limited skills. Consequently, he was forced to leave his job and accept state disability.

The drastic reduction in Gary's income forced his wife, Karen, to seek employment outside the home, a step they had long resisted. Both of them believed it was important for Karen to remain home with their three small children, at least until they entered grade school. Now their dream of "traditional family life" is put on hold until Gary can find a job that pays enough to meet their expenses. Of course, such a prospect seems unlikely in the near future since there is not much demand for unskilled labor, especially at the salary he had been earning.

Gary fights discouragement, especially with Christmas approaching. For the first time ever, the Randall household will be on the receiving end of Christmas goodwill, rather than one of those giving to others. Although Gary knows there is nothing wrong with taking charity, it still hurts. He wants so much to buy the toys the kids hope for and the new dress his wife pretends not to admire, but he can't. Once proud of his role as provider, Gary now struggles with feelings of worthlessness.

Life can throw us curves that alter our dreams and expectations. We can be caught off guard by physical injury, job loss, or any of a hundred other unexpected events. Sometimes carefully planned goals are devastated by the painful realities of life.

ONE DESIRE

Ever since she was a small girl, Cathy remembers wanting nothing more in life than to get married and have children—lots of children. At age twenty-six she finally became a wife, at age thirty-two she still hasn't become a mother. Despite years of treatment from specialists and several surgeries, she is unable to have children. Cathy is infertile.

Cathy has experienced the thrill of discovering she was expecting a child only to be denied the joy of holding her own baby to her breast. On two different occasions Cathy miscarried. The doctors gave her all the hope in the world for carrying both babies to term, intensifying the agonizing disappointment when she lost them.

When she looks around, it seems that every other woman in the world is able to have a baby, including those who don't want or seem unworthy of the privilege. Millions of babies are aborted each year. others are born to women who sell their bodies for drugs, while still others are born to couples who will never see the inside of a church! Why, Cathy wonders, is she denied the joy of motherhood?

Mother's Day and Christmas are particularly difficult times for her. The whole of society celebrates those who have had children in May, and those who are children in December. Raised in a family of six kids, Cathy now has plenty of nieces and nephews to love. But there is a tremendous difference between holding your sister's baby and holding your own. Sometimes it is easier to avoid them than to be with them. Although she knows it is wrong, Cathy struggles with bitterness.

For many, it seems as though the single most desired objective in life is the very thing they are never able to do. This void is felt more deeply when others, including those who seem undeserving, are able to attain it with little difficulty. When the denied objective is something that seems to be part of the natural life cycle or is perceived to be an inherent right, bitterness can be an unpleasant outgrowth of the frustration.

THE PEOPLE IN OUR LIVES

As the saying goes, no man is an island. Every person impacts others in one way or another. Sometimes that impact is unwelcome.

BETRAYED

For more than ten years, James served in the dual role of music minister and associate pastor in a small Baptist church. He had developed an outstanding music program that rivaled those of much larger congregations, and his concern for people prompted significant growth. On several occasions he declined higher paying job offers from bigger, more established churches so that he could continue investing in the lives of those he had grown to love.

James and his wife, Gail, who was also active in the ministry of the church, saw quite a few changes in the membership over the years. When they began serving on the staff, the entire congregation was no more than a handful of the faithful. Years later, after much hard work and sacrifice, the church had grown so large that it became necessary to build a new five-hundred-seat sanctuary in order to hold services. The largest contributing factor to that growth, most everyone agreed, was the presence and loving diligence of James and Gail. Most of the people who attended and supported the church were attracted to its outreach due primarily to the sacrifices made by James and his family.

After a few years of church growth, the head pastor decided to retire. As a simple, country preacher, he knew that he was ill-equipped to lead what was quickly becoming a mega-church outreach. Not wanting to stand in the way of the ministry's continued expansion, he recommended that the church find a new senior pastor. After investigating several candidates, the membership called Dr. Fred Cummings, a seminary graduate with years of church growth experience.

It wasn't long after the change in leadership before James sensed a new attitude toward his work at the church—one of suspicion rather than appreciation. There were several differences in ministry philosophy between James and Dr. Cummings, but the tension seemed to relate more specifically to insecurity on the part of the new senior pastor. He perceived James as a threat to his leadership, rather than as a source of support. Months of tension and distrust between the two culminated in an ugly confrontation and an eventual parting of the ways.

Feeling unappreciated and betrayed, James left the church to which he had dedicated so much of his life. After more than a decade of service and sacrifice, he was tossed aside without regard for what he had done for the congregation. How could such injustice occur in the realm of ministry?

Two people equally dedicated to a cause, even to the point of personal sacrifice, can experience serious conflict trying to work together. Stories abound of people who think they've been burned by an insensitive and power-hungry board member, boss, colleague, or even friend.

People such as James have every reason to feel victimized by the actions of other people. Whether due to personal or philosophical differences, interpersonal conflict can be traumatic. It is particularly painful when the hoped for "justice" never occurs.

BLOWN OVER

I grew up in the suburbs of Detroit. Like every other homeowner in the neighborhood, we had a small yard with a few trees planted here and there to break up the monotony. Being in a four-season state meant that every autumn the leaves changed colors and died. Although the colors were beautiful for a few weeks, eventually those dead leaves had to be raked into piles and burned, and it was frequently my job to do it. After some initial moaning over the stress and strain of manual labor, I eventually took on the task with pride. I was going to have the best-looking yard on that otherwise identical street.

Unfortunately, our next-door neighbor didn't take the same pride in his lawn. Even more unfortunate, we lived downwind of him. Consequently, when the wind blew, I not only had to rake our leaves but his as well. If he would have worked as hard as I did to keep his lawn raked, my life would have been easier.

In much the same way, many of us find ourselves impacted by the messes others make. We work hard all day to keep our lives neatly raked, only to find a mess the next morning due to someone else's irresponsibility.

Lisa has difficulty identifying with her pastor's series on building a healthy family. She has a family, but it is far from healthy. Lisa's husband, Mark, is an alcoholic, and she worries about her two sons. She wants the boys to become responsible young men, but their model of manhood is less than ideal. Despite her efforts to keep the boys in church and teach them right and wrong, she fears that they will follow in their father's irresponsible footsteps.

There were plenty of warning signs before Lisa married Mark that problems could develop. He was not very responsible and drank a bit too much. But he had a stable job, and her family pushed them to get married. After all, a twenty-nine-year-old girl can't be too picky! Now Lisa wishes she had been more patient.

Three months into the marriage communication ended. Two months later Lisa discovered that she was expecting twins. Realizing that they were having serious problems, Lisa's uncle offered to pay for a divorce. Lisa declined because she believed it would be wrong. She hoped that things would improve once there were children in the home.

Years later, things still haven't improved. As quickly as Lisa earns the money to feed and clothe the kids, Mark spends it at the bar. It's so unfair! While he enjoys his buddies and booze at the local tavern, she and the boys suffer in silence. Despite Lisa's efforts to make life for the boys as normal as possible, Mark's leaves keep blowing onto her lawn.

The messes made by others can and will create difficult obstacles to advancement in life. For some, things seem so bad that the hope of moving forward has been replaced with a desire to maintain the status quo.

OUR HUMAN TENDENCIES

Although most of us openly acknowledge the difficulties caused by past experiences, present circumstances, and the actions of other people, admitting our own failures and weaknesses is something we'd rather not do. None of us consciously sets out to become a failure or a fool. Yet we do exactly that when we neglect to consider seriously the impact of our attitudes and actions. Like it or not, the natural tendencies of human nature slide toward the lowest common denominator. We all desire to go up, but the escalator is headed down.

Our son, Joshua Kyle, is the joy of our lives and the source of our exhaustion. We feed him, change him, carry him, play with him, and, of course, love him. But he couldn't care less about our needs. He doesn't sit up at night wondering if he has hurt our feelings or whether or not we had enough to eat during the dinner hour that he spent screaming. He only cares that we pick up, put down, feed, change, and play with him at his command.

All of us started life in that state. Human nature is characterized by two adjectives: selfishness and ignorance. We don't know anything beyond our own needs, nor do we care. Unfortunately, these basic human tendencies do not disappear when we turn two, or even twenty. We are stuck with them for life, and unless we recognize that, we will fall into the same traps over and over throughout our lives.

Selfishness shows its ugly head in many different shapes and sizes. First, we can be very demanding, often by claiming "our rights." Second, we show our self-centeredness through self-preservation. We avoid pain at all costs or refuse to accept responsibility for our errors by deflecting blame to someone else, even to the point of self-deception.

Ignorance stays with us for as long as we allow it. Without discipline and diligence, the mind wastes away. We remain infantile in our understanding and attitudes. Left unchanged, our tendency to "go with the flow" will carry us in the wrong direction.

Perhaps the most frustrating aspect of our fallen nature is that even when we want to do right we continue doing wrong. The destructive cycle of sin can ensnare us easily. Our advancement is subverted by our own actions.

SELF-SUBVERSION

Steve was raised in a strong Christian family that faithfully attended church at least three times a week. The principles of

God's Word were deeply ingrained in his life from childhood. His greatest desire was to please the Lord, and he looked forward to eventually working in full-time ministry.

Upon completing high school Steve was able to attend a Christian college where he received the training necessary to fulfill his ministerial ambitions. Yet something began to wear away the joy that had characterized Steve's otherwise victorious life. Although his heartfelt desire was to live a pure life, impure thoughts continually bombarded his mind.

Beginning with occasional indulgence in soft pornographic literature, the progression of the flesh led him into harder and harder material. Steve wanted to be free from the enslavement of sexual addiction, but the pull of desire had him hooked. Regardless of how often he confessed and pleaded with God to cleanse him, Steve's lust continued to overwhelm him.

Steve never revealed his inner turmoil to those around him because he felt a responsibility to be an example for the "weaker Christians" to whom he was ministering. Unable to talk to anyone about his struggle, Steve felt all alone. He couldn't even talk to God anymore, certain that the Lord was tired of hearing the same promises of repentance over and over again.

Overtaken by guilt and self-hatred, Steve abandoned his dream of going into the ministry. He became angry at the God he once loved for failing to provide deliverance. Steve now lives alone, trapped in a lagoon of depression.

Whether sexual compulsion, alcohol addiction, uncontrolled anger, laziness, or any number of individual weaknesses, our human tendencies as fallen creatures can lead us to subvert our own advancement unintentionally. In many cases, we are not even aware of the specific actions, habits, or attitudes that create the current of resistance in our lives. All we know is that we can't seem to gain freedom from the cycle of self-defeat.

FACING THE CURRENT

On the river of life, there are no exceptions. Even for Christians, it's difficult. Recognizing this truth early is invaluable. In order to overcome the inevitable obstacles, we must first honestly face the specific downstream currents unique to our individual lives. If we deny or ignore them, they will carry us away. If we confront and resist them, we are on the way to moving upstream.

Though some currents are common to all, such as our basic human weaknesses, unique sources of resistance afflict every person's life. You may identify with one of those mentioned in this chapter, or you may have entirely different difficulties that create your downstream drift. Either way, it is essential that you face your particular current head-on and begin going against the flow.

What good does it do to focus on the negative? Isn't it better to keep a positive, victorious attitude? Although there is a place for finding the silver lining, recognizing the cloud is also a necessary part of developing an honest, healthy approach to life. Scott Peck, in the opening chapter of his best-selling book *The Road Less Traveled,* put it like this:

> Life is difficult. This is a great truth, one of the greatest truths. It is a great truth because once we truly see this truth, we transcend it. Once we truly know that life is difficult—once we truly understand and accept it—then life is no longer difficult. Because once it is accepted, the fact that life is difficult no longer matters.
>
> Most do not fully see this truth that life is difficult. Instead they moan more or less incessantly, noisily or subtly, about the enormity of their problems, their burdens, and their difficulties as if life were generally easy, as if life *should* be easy.[1]

Once we realize that life is difficult, it removes our sense of isolation. If life is hard for *everyone,* we are not alone in our struggle. Though the particulars may be different for each of us, the reality of personal struggle applies to all. My struggles may be completely different from yours, but we share the common experience of difficulty in life.

BOTTOM LINE

We all desire to head upstream, but the currents of life are pulling us downstream. Past experiences, present circumstances, other people, and our own tendencies as fallen human beings create serious resistance to our advancement in life. Until we recognize that fact, we will be unable to begin the long trek toward personal growth and upstream living.

2

Upstream Ambition

Never forget that only dead fish swim with the stream.
Malcolm Muggeridge

Ever since that first visit during their honeymoon, my parents have loved Niagara Falls. Consequently, our annual family vacations frequently included a few days watching that magnificent marvel of the world.

Standing near the edge of the falls and watching the water rush past and drop hundreds of feet is awe inspiring. It would be difficult to find a more sensational display of force in all of nature. Fear grips your heart if you imagine yourself trapped in the current of the mighty Niagara River, unable to avert the plunge toward certain death.

If you leave the edge of the falls and head upriver, you will eventually reach a more peaceful setting. Though the current still exists, it is much less strong. You may even see small fishing boats on the river going about their business as if they were on any other river. One major difference, however, is the knowledge of what lies further downstream.

Those who have visited Niagara may recall hearing the story of a man and his two young children who neglected to take the necessary precautions and were inadvertently pulled by the current toward the dangerous rapids and the falls. Oblivious to what was happening, they let their small rowboat be pulled into the rushing rapids of the river. The turbulent water capsized the tiny boat before the father was able to get it to safety. The three were carried over the falls.

The two children miraculously survived the incident, and their rescue from the lower river was captured on film. It serves as a reminder for those upstream not to passively accept the pull of the current.

Many of us are pulled toward destruction by minimizing the significance of the current or by ignoring its danger altogether. Personal growth, healthy relationships, and realistic goals are sacrificed on the altars of denial and self-pity. We passively accept our fate, claiming that it is impossible or futile to actively resist the forces of the current.

WHAT'S UPSTREAM?

Few of us are completely satisfied with our present status in life, and perhaps that is good. The moment we stop growing, we stop truly living. Life should be a continuous process of learning, stretching, and improving. There is a measure of discontent in each of us that reveals our common ambition to be further upstream. How we respond to it can determine whether or not we will actually get there.

This "upstream ambition" exposes itself in a deeply felt desire for something that presently seems out of reach. For some it may be as basic as career advancement or financial security. For others it could be an intense yearning for relational harmony or spiritual understanding. Regardless of the specific need, the longing remains until resolution is achieved.

Each individual must identify for himself precisely what it means to be upstream. It would be impossible to provide a universal definition of this goal due to the many variables in the river. However, some common themes can be used to provide a general description. Upstream living includes:

- The ability to develop and maintain healthy, constructive relationships with God, your family, and friends
- Growing spiritually, professionally, and intellectually on a consistent basis
- Personal integrity and financial discipline, as well as the rewards associated with each

In short, it is those positive aspects of life that every person hopes to realize to one degree or another but which few seem to attain. The pull of the current seems to prevent most of us from reaching those simple but significant life goals.

PASSIVE ACCEPTANCE

Why do some people make it upstream, yet others do not? Many who face immense obstacles manage to reach calmer waters, sailing past those facing less severe opposition. Could it be that the former have learned to resist the current, whereas the latter are passively accepting its pull?

DENIAL

Charles was raised in a dysfunctional family. His father, a preacher, had serious emotional problems that caused him to abuse his family verbally and physically. Despite a "health and wealth" theology proclaimed from the pulpit, the family was materially poor and emotionally sick. The scars run deep in Charles.

It is evident to everyone who knows Charles that painful issues are still unresolved in his life, but he refuses to accept the desperately needed balm of healing. Rather than acknowledging and confronting his pain, Charles "claims the promise" of Isaiah 53:5: "And by his wounds we are healed." He takes offense when others try to draw out the details of his past. "All that self-centered introspection is for those without hope," he says, "not for the children of God!" By refusing to look back, however, Charles is preventing himself from moving forward.

We frequently minimize or ignore serious obstacles in our lives under the guise of "victorious Christian living." Rather than honestly acknowledge the difficulties, past or present, that work against us, we pretend they don't exist. But denying problems only intensifies them, and the flow of the river carries us further downstream.

"POOR ME"

Whereas one extreme is to ignore the current of life, the other is to use its pull as an excuse for inactivity. Certainly, some of us have very difficult sources of resistance. But we subvert our own advancement when we see ourselves as helpless victims of circumstance.

Whether because we belong to a racial minority, have little money, or are from a legalistic church, many of us consider ourselves exempt from responsibility for our choices and actions. After all, how can I properly relate to my wife if my dad was a poor example of a husband? How can I become a successful businessman when I don't have a wealthy family to back me?

Rather than finding our identity in Christ, we find it in being an adult child of an alcoholic or the product of a dysfunctional family or any number of labels. These labels let others know that our situation is different and that we can't be expected to function as everyone else does. We cling to our rights and even claim certain privileges based upon what we are "owed" in reparation for what we have suffered or lacked.

We all know people who refuse to let go of anger and bitterness toward their inadequate or abusive parents. Many join support groups to discuss their struggles with others who have experienced similar pain. Others undergo prolonged counseling, repeatedly rehashing the wounds of their past. Yet, few seem to move beyond a victimization mentality into the freedom of personal responsibility. Why? Could it be that we do not really *want* to deal with the issues but rather have a subconscious desire to gain control and power by remaining a "societal victim" in need of special understanding?

A "poor me" mentality can have serious consequences. Rather than holding ourselves accountable for what we do with our lives, we hold our parents, church, or even God responsible for our lack of advancement and growth. Consequently, we never move beyond a self-centered bitterness that blinds us to our opportunities. Although self-pity may feel good for a time and may even be necessary as part of a grieving period, wallowing in it ensures our drift downstream.

"BAIL ME OUT, JESUS"

Susan and her fourteen-year-old daughter, Nycole, have been in constant conflict for years. They just can't seem to get along. A wall has gone up between them, and Susan is losing hope for a loving, normal relationship.

Susan remembers experiencing much the same situation with her own mother while she was growing up. They said some pretty ugly things and never resolved them. Even now their visits are uncomfortable because of the tension. Susan vowed that she would never be like her mother, that she and her daughter would be best of friends. But Nycole says and does many irritating things, making it very difficult. Susan loves Nycole, but she has difficulty liking her!

Although they try to work things out, Susan finds herself struggling with bitterness toward her daughter. Her dream of an ideal relationship is continually thwarted by Nycole's stubborn and self-centered ways. Why can't she be more like the other young ladies at church who get along so well with their mothers?

Susan asks others to join her in prayer for Nycole. She wants the Lord to deal with the rebellious and selfish attitudes in her daughter. After all, only He can touch her heart and bring harmony to their home.

It is easy for Christians to fall into a "Bail me out, Jesus" mentality. Rather than honestly deal with the relational conflicts in our lives, we ask the Lord to "fix" the other person. Susan, like many others, refuses to acknowledge the pattern of conflict and unforgiveness between herself and her mother. As a result, she continues the pattern with her own daughter. Asking the Lord to work on Nycole is much less painful than resolving the conflicts and bitterness between herself and her own mother—or is it?

"FIGHT THE GOOD FIGHT"

Another common avoidance maneuver is to take up the cause of helping others who struggle with the same issue we do. Uniquely qualified to address the needs of those who share similar pains, we march forward under the guise of compassion. Conveniently, we are so busy helping others work through their conflicts that there is no time to deal honestly with our own.

Carol faithfully attends a Bible-teaching church, actively witnesses to those in her neighborhood, leads a Bible study in her home, and works at the local crisis pregnancy center on week-ends. She also has three small children and a deeply troubled marriage.

Bob, Carol's husband, has never "taken spiritual leadership" in the home, and she feels responsible to keep their Christian wit-ness strong. His lack of initiative with family devotions and other spiritual activities causes her to resent him. If only he were more like the pastor, then their marriage would improve.

Bob just wishes she would spend more time at home. She acts as if her Christian "chores" are more important than their marriage. He takes the family to church, works hard to provide for them, and does his best to be sensitive to Carol's needs. But no matter how hard he tries, he can't seem to earn her respect.

Despite the fact that she left Bob emotionally years ago, Carol is concerned that her marriage stay together. It would destroy her Christian witness if there was a divorce. The young women in her Bible study look to her as an example of the virtuous woman, and it would devastate them to know of her struggles. Carol hopes that as long as she gives herself to others, the Lord will keep her mar-riage together. Since there is nothing she can do to change Bob, she thinks she should spend her time changing the world.

It is much more exciting to be a crusader who travels the world fighting dragons than to be a palace guard protecting the home front. We can avoid the day-to-day challenges of living by galloping off into the sunset to rescue others. When we return home, however, we may find it in ruin due to neglect.

"IT'S EASIER FOR YOU"

Not long ago I was visiting an old acquaintance who was feeling somewhat sorry for himself because he was unable to find a job to his liking. He was bemoaning the fact that he had never pursued the academic training necessary for the kind of occupa-tions he would enjoy. After encouraging him to attend school on a part-time basis after work in order to reach his goal of profession advancement, I was perplexed at his response. "Oh, I couldn't do that," he explained. "Trying to balance both work and school is tough!" I explained that my wife and I both worked forty-hour jobs while we were full-time students in order to finish college. To that he responded, "Well, that kind of thing comes easier to you. It would be too difficult for me."

Neither my wife nor I remembers that period being "easier" for us than for anyone else. Working until midnight every night and waking at 6:00 A.M. every morning to go to class certainly seemed difficult at the time. Cramming for exams while downing a breakfast bagel didn't *feel* all that easy. We did it because we were committed to the goal of finishing school, not because we were having fun.

Those who have overcome obstacles in life and moved further upstream would seem to be the most qualified to advise others who face similar hurdles. But sometimes individuals who are downstream do not allow others to provide direction and counsel. Perceiving that the "upstream class" is unable to truly understand their struggles, they turn to other frustrated "downstreamers" for mutual sympathy and support. Consequently, those who have successfully overcome the obstacles are disqualified by their success.

"That's easy for you to say. You've made it!"

"You just don't understand how bad it is."

"It must be easier for you."

Those and other phrases communicate the same basic message: "I am an exception to the norm. I wish I were upstream, but I'm not. And since you are, your life must not be as complex or difficult as mine."

Such comments ignore the fact that difficulty is one of the few commonalities of life. Again, the particular struggles may differ from one individual to the next, but the fact of hardship is certain for all. Not since the Garden of Eden has smooth sailing been the norm. Life is not easy, and if we expect it to be so, we are in for a rough ride. Remember the promise Jesus made: "In this world you will have trouble. But take heart! I have overcome the world" (John 16:33).

Try as we may, we will not change the hardships of life by screaming at them or blaming them or hoping they will disappear. One of the first requirements of mental health is accepting those things in life that cannot be changed. Adversity is one of those certainties.

The fact that others have successfully overcome the same obstacles we face should be a source of inspiration to us. We should also heed the directives of those who are further upstream than we are. They have been where we are, and we hope to get where they are. By suggesting that our plight is more difficult or in some way unique, we are actually using an avoidance technique to keep from confronting life's obstacles. If the advice from those who have made it seems difficult or painful, we brush it off as irrelevant to our situation. In the process, we forfeit the advantages of experienced coaching for the "comfort" of feeling justified in our inactivity.

ACTIVE RESISTANCE

Those who deny the existence of the current or use it as an excuse for inactivity or avoid facing it for whatever reasons actually surrender to its pull. The desire to be upstream remains unfulfilled because we are unwilling to do what is necessary to get there.

Several steps must be taken to begin the process of active resistance. First, we must honestly recognize the particular obstacles that create our unique current of resistance. Until we do so, we are living in denial and cannot confront the sources of our downstream drift.

Second, we must come to grips with the reality that no one else can move us upstream. Only the person in the boat can start paddling against the flow. Doing so, however, is no easy task. It requires that we take personal responsibility for our own situation, regardless of how severe our particular currents may be. We cannot alter the direction of life's river, but we can change the direction we are moving by facing our boat upstream and starting to row.

Finally, we must take personal responsibility for the direction of our life from today forward, regardless of the obstacles. Whether we are dealing with past experiences that created painful memories or current circumstances that must be overcome, it is our individual responsibility to face them. If people in our lives seem to be pushing us downstream, it is up to us to confront or forgive them where needed. If human weaknesses lead us into self-subversive activities or attitudes, we must seek the help and develop the discipline necessary to gain victory. We cannot passively wait for others to fix our problem areas. If we don't do the rowing, the boat won't move.

The common error is to make *being* upstream our aim. But that goal can never be attained. Once we have advanced to the next status, our sights are set further upstream, and a new objective is defined. However, if we make *moving* upstream the goal, consistent advancement and personal growth are their own reward.

When the desire to be upstream is matched by the effort to move upstream, responsible living is the result. When that becomes our normal mode of existence, success is inevitable. Success is defined not as attaining every temporal desire but as glorifying God by becoming all that we can as people made in His image.

BOTTOM LINE

Yes, life is difficult. We must recognize that there will always be obstacles to our growth and success. At the same time, however, we must hold ourselves accountable for actively going against the flow. Our only alternative is to let the pull of the current drag us further and further downstream toward failure and disillusionment. There is a paddle in every boat, and it is called personal responsibility. Each of us must choose to pick it up and start rowing!

Section Two
AGAINST THE FLOW

*God's plan includes equipping His people
to go against the flow in a fallen world
through a lifestyle of
responsibility, wisdom, and success.*

3
Responsible Living

Responsibility is the thing people dread most of all.
Yet it is the one thing in the world that develops us.
Frank Crane

The clock radio blares at precisely 5:30 A.M., beckoning me to face another day. Requiring only a split second to rationalize away the benefits of morning exercise, I slap the snooze button, hoping to steal a few extra minutes of sleep. But the knowledge that I must eventually pull back the covers and start my daily routine ruins an otherwise perfect moment. Rather than fight the inevitable, I roll out of bed and begin another tedious day of toil.

What is it that gets me out of bed in the morning? It certainly isn't the anticipation of my daily shower and shave. Neither am I always thrilled about going to work. I had a job during college where I spent eight-hour shifts painting the heads of silver screws brown. There were definitely other things I would rather have been doing! Yet I went to work every day with full knowledge that I was going to be bored silly. Why? What makes any of us choose the mundane and necessary over the fun and frivolous?

In contrast, what is it that causes some to neglect the most basic activities of wholesome living? One man works sixty hours per week to provide the basic necessities for his family, whereas another spends a mere thirty hours on the job and drinks away his paycheck. A woman who was mistreated as a child wallows in pain and bitterness, whereas another who was more severely abused lives a healthy, productive life. What makes the difference?

I believe the difference lies in whether or not one understands and is committed to responsible living. Those who hold themselves accountable for their own choices and attitudes move upstream on the river of life; those who refuse to be held accountable allow themselves to be pulled downstream. These two opposing lifestyles could be identified as *responsible* and *irresponsible.*

Are you thriving in your workplace? Does your financial situation reflect discipline and careful planning? Do you find yourself growing spiritually as well as intellectually on a consistent basis? Are your relationships with family members and friends peaceful and constructive?

To the extent that we are unable to answer those questions in the affirmative, we are living with a measure of irresponsibility in our lives. It may not be that we are generally irresponsible people, but we have made choices and established patterns that result in unproductive consequences. Thus, all of us, to one degree or another, fall into both lifestyle categories. Our goal is to identify and reinforce the responsible choices and actions and eliminate the irresponsible ones.

When using the term *irresponsible,* I do not mean simple childishness. After all, kids have it in their job descriptions to mess up every now and then. What child doesn't leave his clothes on the floor, spill his milk, fail to brush his teeth, or forget to flush? Even adults do things from time to time that are just plain dumb and could be labeled irresponsible on that level. Yet, that is vastly different from a mind-set and lifestyle of self-defeat.

RESPONSE-ABILITY

Just looking at the word *responsibility* provides a rather simple but profound understanding. We have the ability to choose our response—*response-ability.* Unlike the animals, man is made in God's own image. Consequently, we are not driven by instinct, nor must we give in to our natural impulses. We are able to decide how we will respond to each situation, person, and urge that we face. We cannot change the fact that life is tough, but we have been given the capacity to choose our attitudes and actions, enabling us to rise above our circumstances.

Having the ability to choose our response to difficulty is one thing; doing so in a constructive manner is another. We often respond in harmful and self-defeating ways, rather than positive ones.

I was raised in a family of seven children, six boys and one girl. I have fond memories of the days when all nine of us would gather around the dinner table, thank the Lord for the food, then dig in. I learned early that you had to get while the getting was good, or you didn't get much at all. My mom made plenty to go around, but if you were the slight bit complacent about the evening's selection, my older brothers were glad to relieve you of your portion. Thus, I discovered a profound truth for living: Take what you are given, or you may find yourself with nothing at all.

Reality does not change to fit our preferences or expectations. But we can change our expectations to fit reality. We are all handed a portion of life, difficulties and all, and we must accept what we are given and make the best of it. Complaining about our lot and wishing for a bigger, better, or tastier selection does no good.

Life does dish out some pretty distasteful situations. But unless we are willing to take personal responsibility for our lives and choose a positive response to those challenges, we will subvert our own advancement and character development.

God's Will?

One way we avoid taking personal responsibility for our choices and actions is by pulling God into the picture. Many a foolish decision has been made under the guise of "the Lord's direction." The best way to fulfill your agenda is to claim divine guidance in your decision-making process. To quiet skeptics, just use the old line "I've prayed about this, and I sense the Lord's leading." After all, who's going to second-guess God?

During my college years I knew several students who would drop out of school during the semester because, they claimed, the Lord was leading them to do so. The next semester, however, the Lord led them back. The cycle would continue until folks began asking God to make up His mind.

Pastor Davis was a strong leader with grand visions for his church. He spent his first several years as pastor convincing the congregation that it would be wise to move out of the old city into a nicer area for church growth. There was just one problem; the church was rather small and money very tight. In order to buy property and build a new auditorium, they would need to raise several hundred thousand dollars. But Pastor Davis had a plan.

Convinced that the Lord was leading him, Pastor Davis arranged a deal with the local bank. If the individual members of the congregation would be willing to take personal loans adding up to enough for the down payment on the new property, the bank would make the loan necessary to obtain it. Although the church didn't have a large enough budget to handle the monthly payment, the bank was willing to take the risk since it was certain to make money from the personal loans taken out by the members.

The big fund-raising day arrived, and the entire congregation gathered to execute the pastor's plan for moving the church. After a rather emotional plea by Pastor Davis, the members began making pledges to what they understood to be God's plan for moving the church. One by one, people of all ages and financial status stood to testify of what size loan God was leading them to take. Many, caught up in the excitement of it all, took on more debt than they could possibly repay. But the intense pressure to have faith in the Lord to meet the need, coupled with the inspirational testimonies of sacrifice on the part of others in the congregation, made it difficult to hold back.

One struggling college student committed to take on a $3,000 loan, and another pledged $5,000. "When the Lord leads you to do something," one of them said, "you can't say no!" Both eventually found it necessary to drop out of school until they could pay off the debt.

By the end of the meeting nearly every member had signed loan papers, the individuals in the congregation were financially strapped, and the church had taken on a loan it couldn't afford. But, much to Pastor Davis's delight, the goal necessary to move the church was met. The "faith" demonstrated by his people was an inspiration, and he was certain that the Lord would bless their commitment in the coming years.

It wasn't long before making payments on the new building became impossible. The pastor tried everything to keep from losing the property, including bond issues and convincing several of the members to donate the equity in their homes as collateral for a new church loan. Eventually the bank foreclosed on the church, and they were forced to move out of their lovely new building.

Frustrated, Pastor Davis put the blame on the church body because "only 10 percent of the people in this congregation tithe!" If the members had given as they should have, the church would be "where the Lord wanted them to be." Neither the pastor nor the membership ever stopped to consider the fact that taking on heavy debt is directly contrary to biblical principles of finance. Could it be that it was not God directing them but their own desires and emotional impulses?

It is difficult to be honest about the choices we make. Rather than "I decided to . . . " we say, "God directed me to . . . " When things don't work out as we had hoped, we point the finger of blame at lack of faith or disobedience to God's plan. We rarely stop to consider whether the decision itself was unwise.

Seeking direction from the Lord is certainly appropriate, but making choices is ultimately our responsibility. God gives us everything necessary to make wise decisions, then grants us the freedom to make them. Accountability for the direction taken and the resulting consequences, whether good or bad, must be accepted by the one making the choices. Attempting to shift blame elsewhere, be it onto God or other people, is an outgrowth of irresponsibility.

GIVE ME MY RIGHTS!

We have seen a gradual change over the past several decades in our society from emphasizing individual responsibility to emphasizing, almost glorifying, individual rights. We seem to have replaced the perspective of "It's my responsibility" with one that says, "It's your fault!" If things fall apart, there is always someone at whom we can point an accusing finger.

This tendency can be seen in the workplace, in governmental policies, in civil disputes, in family conflicts, and even in the church. "Give me my rights!" is the battle cry of a new generation. This emphasis may become a primary source of our individual and corporate downfall.

Stay home from work just one afternoon, and you will see numerous television advertisements telling you of your "right" to just compensation for stress at work. A slick lawyer, who claims concern for your well being, says, "Call 1-800-SUE-THEM, and we'll get you what you deserve." Our courts are overburdened, and insurance companies are raising rates out of sight. Most unfortunate, however, is the societal perception that an honest day's pay for an honest day's work just isn't good enough anymore!

Obviously, individual rights are crucial to a free society and essential for personal advancement. But when they are emphasized to the exclusion of individual responsibility, the consequences are tragic. Roger Conner, executive director of Washington's liberal American Alliance for Rights & Responsibilities, provided insightful commentary on this problem in a recent *Time* article:

> I have this image of human beings as porcupines, with rights as their quills. When the quills are activated, people can't touch each other. The R word in our language is responsibility, and it has dropped from the policy dialogue in America. A society can't operate if everyone has rights and no one has responsibilities.[1]

All of us, to one degree or another, hold to certain "rights" in order to avoid taking personal responsibility for our situation. We may feel the right to get even with someone who has hurt us or the right to hold on to bitterness for past disappointments and pain. The thought of letting someone "off the hook" by forgiving him is inconceivable. Consequently, we remain victims to our own aggravation.

If anyone ever had reason to be bitter about past wrongs it was the Old Testament character Joseph. His ten older brothers stripped him of his favorite clothes, threw him into a pit, and left him for dead. Then, overtaken with momentary feelings of compassion, they decided to sell him into Egypt as a slave rather than let him die. With cash in hand and grins on their faces, they ignored his tearful pleas for mercy and watched the caravan ride off with young, frightened Joseph strapped to the back of a cart. Turning toward home, they knew they'd never have to mess with him again.

Joseph was sold as a common slave to a bigwig officer in Pharaoh's guard named Potiphar. Far from his homeland where his father and mother had catered to his every need, Joseph was now the lowest member of the lowest class in Potiphar's household. Not realizing that he could have wallowed in his recent trauma, Joseph decided to glorify his God despite his circumstances. Consequently, God rewarded his integrity and hard work, eventually placing him in charge of Potiphar's entire household.

> From the time he put him in charge of his household and of all that he owned, the Lord blessed the household of the Egyptian because of Joseph. The blessing of the Lord was on everything Potiphar had, both in the house and in the field. So he left in Joseph's care everything he had; with Joseph in charge, he did not concern himself with anything except the food he ate. (Genesis 39:5-6)

Things were finally looking up! That is, until Mrs. Potiphar entered the picture. Joseph was a rather handsome young man, and Mrs. P. liked them that way. She pursued him repeatedly, only to be slapped in the face by Joseph's integrity. As politely as possible, he ran out of the room whenever she entered. Eventually, in her anger, Mrs. P. accused him of attacking her. So Potiphar threw him into prison.

Sitting in a cold dungeon, Joseph again had every reason to become bitter. After all, he had attempted to do what was right in every situation, only to be rewarded with misfortune and abuse. Instead, he took personal responsibility for his own attitude and continued his pattern of doing his best regardless of the circumstances. As a result, the upstream trend of Joseph's life continued.

> So the warden put Joseph in charge of all those held in the prison, and he was made responsible for all that was done there. The warden paid no attention to anything under Joseph's care, because the Lord was with Joseph and gave him success in whatever he did. (Genesis 39:22-23)

Again, things were looking up. However, even the top job in a prison isn't all that glamorous. You can bet Joseph would have chosen to be a free man. Finally, his chance to get out came.

Pharaoh's personal baker and butler were thrown into the same prison as Joseph, apparently after serving a bad meal. Each

of them had a rather troubling dream, which the Lord enabled
Joseph to interpret. The butler was given good news. He would be
back in his favored position within three days. The baker's news
was much worse: "Within three days Pharaoh will lift off your
head and hang you on a tree. And the birds will eat away your
flesh" (Genesis 40:19).

So Joseph asked the butler for one small favor.

> But when all goes well with you, remember me and show me kind-
> ness; mention me to Pharaoh and get me out of this prison. For I was
> forcibly carried off from the land of the Hebrews, and even here I have
> done nothing to deserve being put in a dungeon. (Genesis 40:14-15)

Two years later, Joseph was still sitting in a dungeon. As is
typically the case, when the butler made it big, he forgot the little
people who had helped him along. Again, Joseph bore the brunt
of another's misdeed.

Finally, thirteen years after the incident with his ten brothers,
Joseph was freed. When Pharaoh had a troubling dream that no
one could interpret, the butler remembered Joseph and brought
him up to the court to reveal the meaning. Not only did Joseph
provide an interpretation, but he also made a recommendation for
how to balance the coming years of plenty and famine. As had
been his pattern, Joseph gave credit where credit was due and
informed Pharaoh that it was God who had granted the interpretation and wisdom. Consequently, he received a promotion that
made the prison and Potiphar's house pale in comparison.

> So Pharaoh asked them, "Can we find anyone like this man, one in
> whom is the spirit of God?" Then Pharaoh said to Joseph, "Since God
> has made all this known to you, there is no one so discerning and
> wise as you. You shall be in charge of my palace, and all my people
> are to submit to your orders. Only with respect to the throne will I be
> greater than you." So Pharaoh said to Joseph, "I hereby put you in
> charge of the whole land of Egypt." (Genesis 41:38-41)

Now, let's examine Joseph's situation. He had total authority
under Pharaoh to rule the people of Egypt. Anything he wished to
do he could do, including getting even with certain folks who had

done him wrong. The absent-minded butler could have received a painful lesson on forgetfulness. Potiphar, who had thrown Joseph into prison without just cause, was now under his command. Later, when Joseph's ten brothers came to buy grain from Egypt, he could have made them suffer in fear and pain just as they had made him suffer when he was a child. Rather than cling to his "right" to get even, however, Joseph forgave. Why?

The answer is evident in Joseph's pronouncement upon revealing his identity to the brothers:

> I am your brother Joseph, the one you sold into Egypt! And now, do not be distressed and do not be angry with yourselves for selling me here, because it was to save lives that God sent me ahead of you. (Genesis 45:4-5)

And later when they feared retribution:

> Don't be afraid. Am I in the place of God? You intended to harm me, but God intended it for good to accomplish what is now being done, the saving of many lives. (Genesis 50:19-20)

Throughout his suffering, mistreatment, and pain, Joseph maintained a perspective of responsible living. He saw God's hand in every situation. Certainly, those who mistreated him did so out of an evil heart and meant it for wrong. But God was able to use painful experiences to develop character in Joseph and to orchestrate a plan for saving the known world from mass starvation. Rather than claim his right to justice, Joseph left it up to God to "settle the score" and chose to forgive that which was unforgivable.

Sometimes we think we have a legitimate right to hold grudges. We fail to remember that "God is in control, and if I let Him, He can use this evil for good in my life." Once we choose to respond in a positive manner, yielding the right to get even, we free ourselves from the destructive bondage of bitterness. We also provide God the opportunity to do great things in our lives.

You see, the question to ask ourselves when responding to any life situation is not, "What is my right?" but rather, "What is my responsibility?" When we emphasize our response to a struggle rather than the struggle itself, we are living in a responsible manner.

PROACTIVE LIVING

Like most adolescents, I struggled with feelings of depression from time to time during my early teen years. Even the most minor frustrations would throw me into a state of introspection about the meaning of it all. *What's the point in trying?* I would ask myself. *This life is just not worth the effort. I'm a failure, no one understands me, and no one cares anyway!*

Although it seemed as though life had lost all meaning, the real reasons for my discouragement were a bit less dramatic, such as losing a game of one-on-one basketball against my buddy or eating too many mini pecan pies for lunch. Still, the way I felt was my reality, regardless of the way things actually were.

My mom could always tell when I was feeling low, and she had a special way of making me feel better. Like any sensitive, caring mother, she sent me outside to sweep the garage. Just when I most wanted sympathy and understanding, I was handed a broom. But, believe it or not, that was just what I needed. By the time I had finished the job, I no longer remembered why I had been feeling down.

Although I am not suggesting that we ignore our difficulties by becoming involved in distractions, there is something to be said for allowing positive activity to replace negative introspection. Mom had the wisdom to know that sometimes the thing we least want to do is the very thing we most need to do. By turning my passive introspection into constructive activity, I learned the value of proactive living.

Being proactive means taking personal responsibility for our own lives. It means making choices based upon values, rather than circumstances or feelings. When we live proactively, we do what is best regardless of how we feel. When we live reactively, we do what we feel regardless of what is best.

Responsible living includes choosing to be proactive rather than reactive on the river of life. We move forward, not because it is easy or because it feels good but because our only alternative is moving backward. Once we have begun, however, we find the process much less difficult and the rewards well worth the effort. We could end up with both a positive perspective and a clean garage!

LIMITS

Angela is hopelessly in love. Unlike the men she has dated in the past, Dan is a true gentleman. He treats her with the utmost respect and has shown a sincere desire to build a relationship founded upon mutual commitment and moral purity. Dan also demonstrates an extraordinary amount of responsibility for a young man in his mid-twenties. While the other single guys were indulging in selfish pursuits, he sacrificed his own goals in order to help provide for his rather needy family. He is a man of true integrity and discipline, and Angela hopes they can marry some-day soon. Unfortunately, that may not happen.

Dan's sense of responsibility to his family is holding him back from making a commitment to the woman he loves. Because Dan is the oldest boy, the entire family has looked to him for leadership since his father's death ten years earlier. If he were to leave home, the bills would go unpaid, the house would deteriorate, and his mother would enter a deep depression. Although there are other adult children in the home, Dan's mother has depended on him to provide her with emotional support since losing her husband. By marrying Angela, Dan believes that he would be placing his own desires above his responsibility to the family. Heartbroken, Angela waits for a wedding day that may never come.

Although his motives have been pure, Dan has allowed a misplaced sense of responsibility to lead him into irresponsible behavior. Responsible living includes recognizing the limits. There are many things we are *not* responsible for. We are not ac-countable for fixing the dysfunctional aspects of another person's life or for providing meals for the lazy or for protecting the reck-less. In fact, by doing so, we actually enable others to continue their lives of irresponsibility, which is detrimental to all. Recogniz-ing the limits gives us the freedom to overcome any misplaced sense of duty and begin concentrating on the choices and atti-tudes that truly do belong under our tent of responsibility.

Christians are responsible to demonstrate the love of Christ by reaching out to those who are legitimately disadvantaged and needy. However, we must be careful not to confuse acts of charity for those who *can't* with support for the lifestyle of those who *won't.* There will always be people who will gladly take advantage of our good will. We can be manipulated into believing that it is our duty to meet their physical or emotional needs when in reality we are satisfying their self-defeating desire to avoid the discomfort of personal growth and discipline.

That principle applies to many areas of life. We must identify which things we are accountable for and which things we are not. We are responsible for our response to the circumstances of life, for example, but not for the circumstances themselves. We are responsible for making right choices in a fallen world but not for righting all societal ills. We are responsible for declaring the truth but not for the response of our hearers. Unless we come to grips with the limits of responsibility, the scope of our "mission" can overwhelm us, and we can end up neglecting our true responsibilities after all.

Bottom Line

We have made several observations about what it means to live a responsible lifestyle.

First, we have been given the ability to choose our response to any situation. We are not slaves of instinct; we have the capacity to rise above our circumstances by the grace of God. We can choose to respond to life's inevitable difficulties in a constructive, positive manner, or we can wallow in bitterness and subvert our own advancement.

Second, we must hold ourselves accountable for our own choices. Although it is certainly appropriate to seek direction from the Lord and others, we are responsible for whatever final decisions we make. When we blame others for our own poor choices, we lead ourselves and others into a self-defeating pattern of blame shifting and denial.

Third, we must emphasize individual responsibility over individual rights. When we become caught up in the demand for personal rights, we neglect our responsibility to properly respond to a given situation. Like Joseph, we need to see God's hand in all of life and allow Him to turn even injustices into opportunities for growth.

Fourth, we must live proactively rather than reactively by turning passive introspection into constructive activity. Doing what is best regardless of circumstances or feelings will move us forward on the river of life.

Finally, we must recognize the limits of our personal responsibility. When we feel a duty toward everything and everyone in our path, we can quickly head into irresponsible behavior under the guise of responsible living.

An understanding of and commitment to responsible living is necessary to move us beyond the obstacles of life toward healthy, productive living. It is also the manner by which we can glorify God. Certainly, it takes discipline and hard work to get upstream, but the rewards are well worth the effort.

4
Wisdom Living

A wise man will make more opportunities than he finds.
Francis Bacon

Why should we bother to head upstream in life? After all, aren't Christians supposed to humbly accept whatever comes our way rather than pursue our own advancement? Isn't it inconsistent with our calling to consider temporal concerns?

In order to answer those questions, we need to find the balance between heavenly values and earthly living. God has revealed a plan for us to incorporate both into the Christian life.

THE BIG PICTURE

Throughout history, God has chosen people to fulfill two specific roles in the world. First, they are to articulate the message of redemption, including His loving provision of salvation. Second, they are to model a lifestyle of purpose and wisdom among people with no sense of direction. These two roles are intended to work hand in hand to accomplish the Lord's purposes. However, we frequently fall into the trap of emphasizing one over the other.

It is not difficult to identify which of the two has been neglected by the evangelical community. We spend our energies proclaiming the gospel message through every medium available yet fail to address the practical, everyday aspects of wisdom living. Is it any wonder that the world ignores the message when those of us delivering it are as messed up and irresponsible as those we are trying to convince?

I believe that one of the primary reasons the Christian community has been negligent in its role as a model of responsible living is its failure to understand the principles of living outlined in the Old Testament. We focus so heavily on the gospel message and epistle doctrines that we ignore the wealth of advice for practical living contained in those dusty old volumes known as wisdom literature. By examining their message, however, we can learn what it means to live wisely.

In order to grasp the significance of the truths in the wisdom books, we must go back and examine the context in which they were written. Wisdom living is more than following a formula or listening to a few isolated proverbs. It involves an entire shift in thinking about the principles that govern the world and our role in it as children of God.

THE TENSION

Man has made some marvelous achievements through the creative ingenuity granted him by God. The human mind is incredibly complex and productive, and its potential for good is limitless. But so is its potential for evil. Herein lies the tension of human existence. We have been given all of the tools necessary to live harmonious, productive lives but have been unable to live thus for thousands of years. Why?

Some will immediately exclaim that the reason is man's utter depravity and inability to do anything good. Others will say it is because we have been influenced by negative events, leading us into behavior that is inconsistent with our otherwise good nature. One considers man totally evil and barren, the other considers him entirely good and full of potential. One downplays man's ability to accomplish good, the other expects more than is realistic. Which perspective is correct?

Could it be that both are partially right? The book of Genesis describes man as having two opposing qualities. On one side, he is created in God's image with tremendous potential. On the other side, he is a fallen creature with an evil heart. The tension between the two is constant and, unless it is properly understood, can lead to confusion and disillusionment as we try to understand our dilemma.

CREATION ENDOWMENT

A major investment firm recently popularized a slogan that reflects the spirit, even expectation, of most in our culture: "Americans want to succeed, not just survive!" The drive for success in our society has led to the highest national standard of living in the Western world, some of the greatest scientific discoveries and medical breakthroughs, and worldwide influence known to few other peoples in history.

But Americans are not the only ones with a drive to better themselves and influence the rest of the world. Recent events have demonstrated that, given the chance, every nation will reach farther and higher than was previously imagined. Japan has emerged as an economic superpower just four decades after the devastation of World War II. The European community has reestablished itself as a leading region of financial and cultural influence in the same period of time. Even the Communist world, fed up with the limits placed upon it by a system that discourages ingenuity, has demanded increased opportunity for individual and corporate advancement.

This tendency within every person to better himself when given the chance is an outgrowth of our human nature. Our ability to create a culture and govern our environment was also part of the original design. Let's look at the blueprint as described in the first chapter of Genesis:

> Then God said, "Let us make man in our image, in our likeness, and let them rule over the fish of the sea and the birds of the air, over the livestock, over all the earth, and over all the creatures that move along the ground." So God created man in his own image, in the image of God he created him; male and female he created them. God blessed them and said to them, "Be fruitful and increase in number; fill the earth and subdue it. Rule over the fish of the sea and the birds of the air and over every living creature that moves on the ground." (Genesis 1:26-28)

From day one, God intended for man to rule the earth as His representative. Man was uniquely equipped with the desire and abilities necessary to carry out this mandate of dominion. He was to build a civilization and culture to the glory of God, using his incredible faculties as one created in the likeness of the Creator. This creation endowment includes the ability to reason, invent, build, organize, and develop. So long as man remained in submission to God, his source of direction and purpose, everything would go according to plan.

FALLEN WORLD

The plan encountered a serious setback when man decided that submission to the Almighty was less exciting than being his own god. As described in the third chapter of the book of Genesis, eating the forbidden fruit was not an isolated act of mischief but a deliberate rejection of God's authority and a gesture toward human autonomy. The way in which the tempter framed the issue clarifies the intention: "When you eat of it your eyes will be opened, and you will be like God, knowing good and evil" (Genesis 3:5).

Immediately after the Fall, dramatic changes occurred, none of them good. Peace, pleasure, and progress were no longer the order of the day. They were replaced by strife, toil, and decline. In addition to life's becoming difficult, man became irresponsible. Both Adam and Eve quickly caught on to the art of blame shifting in order to avoid taking personal responsibility for their actions: "The man said, 'The woman you put here with me—she gave me some fruit from the tree, and I ate it.' . . . The woman said, 'The serpent deceived me, and I ate'" (Genesis 3:12-13).

In short, man decided to become master of his own destiny rather than submit to the One who holds the future in His hands. He also threw off the "shackles" of accountability in favor of the "freedom" of irresponsible living.

The first three chapters of Genesis explain the two aspects of humanity that work against one another. First, man has been endowed with the ability and desire to exercise dominion over God's creation. However, by rejecting the plan of the Designer, he lost his direction and became his own enemy. Like a curious child who picks up a loaded gun, mankind is unaware of the dangers of misusing his potent capabilities.

THE PROBLEM

Some would suggest that the human race lost its ability to do anything constructive due to the Fall. However, there is no indication that the basic makeup of man changed when Adam bit into the fruit. His ability did not change, but his objective did. *Rather than build a civilization and culture to the glory of God, man began building to his own glory and exultation.*

It wasn't long after leaving the Garden of Eden that man began his misguided efforts to live apart from God. The results were less than exemplary. In fact, the world became so hopelessly corrupt that it was necessary for God to judge the race with a worldwide flood. Although the offer to escape destruction went out to everyone, only one family decided to obey. Noah and his clan entered an ark and averted death. Mankind was given a fresh opportunity to do it right. But he didn't.

The next major scene in the drama of Genesis is one of the most blatant examples of human arrogance to be found anywhere. God commanded man to be fruitful, multiply, and fill the earth. They were fruitful, and they multiplied, but they didn't fill the earth. In fact, they deliberately did the opposite.

> Now the whole world had one language and a common speech. As men moved eastward, they found a plain in Shinar and settled there. . . . Then they said, "Come, let us build ourselves a city, with a tower that reaches to the heavens, so that we may make a name for ourselves and not be scattered over the face of the whole earth." (Genesis 11:1-4)

In open defiance, man chose to build a civilization to his own glory rather than submit to God's plan. It is important to note that mankind still used his capacity for accomplishment that God granted him at creation. The Lord never removed man's creation endowment, even when he used it for wrong. In fact, God Himself provides a significant commentary on man's corporate ability in the context of this event: "And the Lord said, 'Behold, they are one people, and they all have the same language. And this is what they began to do, and now nothing which they purpose to do will be impossible for them'" (Genesis 11:6, NASB*).

More than any other generation in history, we have had the opportunity to see the accuracy of this statement. The achievements of man over the past century boggle the mind. Imagine the

New American Standard Bible.

reaction of a pre–industrial revolution person who is given the chance to catch a glimpse of today's technology. If televisions, automobiles, airplanes, computers, and indoor toilets don't put him into shock, our advances in medicine, agriculture, and sanitation will. Along with the improvements, however, he would learn of how these technical advancements have been used to execute the Holocaust and to create weapons of mass destruction. Man can do whatever he sets his mind to, and that is the problem.

Apparently to prevent a reoccurrence of mass evil, God dispersed humanity across the earth by confusing their language. "'Come, let us go down and confuse their language so they will not understand each other.' So the Lord scattered them from there over all the earth, and they stopped building the city" (Genesis 11:7-8).

To this day, the wall of multiple languages prevents accomplishments that could come about with full human cooperation. Let's hope that we never fully overcome that obstacle.

Mankind has repeatedly attempted to create a utopian civilization. Yet his efforts have failed because they have been based upon the faulty premise that man can function independent of God. As C. S. Lewis explains:

> That is the key to history. Terrific energy is expended—civilizations are built up—excellent institutions devised; but each time something goes wrong. Some fatal flaw always brings the selfish and cruel people to the top and it all slides back into misery and ruin. In fact, the machine conks. It seems to start up all right and runs a few yards, and then it breaks down. They are trying to run it on the wrong juice. That is what Satan has done to us humans.[1]

Man has used what was intended for good as a means of accomplishing great evil. Why then hasn't God taken away his abilities? Why leave the loaded gun in his hand? It is because God has not abandoned His original plan of a people in submission to His will, using their gifts to create a civilization and culture to His glory.

THE REMEDY

As the curtain closes on the first act of Genesis, anticipation is high. What will God do to remedy the terrible plight of the human race? They have rejected His authority over their lives, abandoned His plan for the world, and used their creation endowment for evil rather than good. Most distressing is the fact that they are unknowingly headed toward self-destruction, both individually and corporately.

Since the Fall, our ability to function according to God's original design for us has been seriously handicapped. Like a person with damaged vision, we are unable to see clearly the dangerous obstacles before us. Though in desperate need of guidance from one with clear sight, we are too proud to admit our need. "I can see just fine!" we convince ourselves, only to stumble into the pitfalls.

In order to prevent us from destroying ourselves, God reaches out to provide the two things necessary to remedy our situation. First, He offers *relationship* with Himself. God is the only one who has clear enough vision to guide our steps. He simply asks us to submit to His direction. In essence, He extends His hand for us to hold as we cross the dangerous street. Second, He offers *revelation* of what steps to take. He tells us when to step up, step down, and when we are approaching danger. It is up to each of us to choose how we will respond to His directives.

In the twelfth chapter of Genesis, the Lord establishes a covenant with a man named Abram. That covenant was an expression of God's desire for relationship with man, as well as man's need for relationship with God. Abram's descendants were to be the people who would finally fulfill God's original plan for man to build a civilization and culture to His glory. In addition, they would demonstrate to the rest of mankind that reaching out for God's hand and submitting to His leading is the basis for wise and successful living.

WISDOM CULTURE

In our generation, the word *wisdom* invokes images of old, bearded men crouched over thick, dusty books contemplating deep but boring hypotheses. We may also categorize wisdom as an academic topic or as the theme for a series of lessons in Sunday school. But using the word *wisdom* in the context of our home, our profession, or our leisure seems inappropriate.

Actually, when properly understood, wisdom is more related to our day-to-day activities than to our intellectual stimulation. Simply defined, *wisdom is being skillful and successful in the art of living*. Many who never got past the sixth grade are more skilled and successful at the art of living than those who have earned Ph.D.s. The way we live on a daily basis is what certifies our level of wisdom, not the number of sheepskins hanging on the wall.

In the ancient world, the term *wisdom* was used primarily to denote technical ability. The label "wise man" was attached to one who possessed a particular skill, such as an artist or a carpenter. If, for example, you wanted to add an addition to your house, you would call the "Wise Guy & Sons" building company to do the work. In turn for their "wisdom," you would pay them a fair wage. Just as being skilled in a particular technical field was valuable, relational skills, political savvy, philosophical insight, and spiritual understanding were in high demand. In fact, many of the ancient Near Eastern kings hired servants with the full-time job of collecting, composing, and compiling wise proverbs and riddles. Wisdom was the in thing!

It is in that cultural context that the Old Testament wisdom literature was penned. King Solomon's collection of insights are contained in the book of Proverbs. The other wisdom books, Ecclesiastes and Job, were also written in that cultural context. All wisdom writings, whether Hebrew or pagan, had a specific objective: to develop the skill of living.

There was a major difference between the pagan nations and the nation of Israel with regard to the pursuit of wisdom: the objective. The primary focus of the population at large was to develop the skill of living in order to achieve individual and corporate success. In keeping with human nature, the lust for wealth, power, and fame were the driving factors. In short, they sought their own glorification and advancement. In Hebrew wisdom literature, however, we find a dramatically different emphasis. Although individual and corporate success were an outgrowth of their wisdom living, the primary objective was to glorify God, and the foundation of understanding was submission to His authority.

And he said to man, "The fear of the Lord—that is wisdom, and to shun evil is understanding." (Job 28:28)

The fear of the Lord is the beginning of knowledge, but fools despise wisdom and discipline. (Proverbs 1:7)

Here is the conclusion of the matter: Fear God and keep his commandments, for this is the whole duty of man. (Ecclesiastes 12:13)

While the world at large was seeking to advance its own agenda, that small group of covenant people was attempting to demonstrate the futility of life apart from God. During the few times that they did it right, everything came together for Israel. During the early reign of Solomon, for example, the kingdoms of the world marveled at the achievements of this nation and its singular purpose of building a civilization and culture to the glory of God.

It is common for evangelical Christians to think poverty and failure are more spiritual than wealth and success. This perception provides a convenient excuse for failing to use our abilities and gifts to their fullest. Yet God gave us the capacity to accomplish great things for a reason. Solomon understood that principle well.

The nation of Israel reached its golden era during the reign of King Solomon. More than any other ruler in the world, Solomon had mastered the skill of living through divinely granted wisdom. His insights and success prompted the admiration of his contemporaries.

God gave Solomon wisdom and very great insight, and a breadth of understanding as measureless as the sand on the seashore. Solomon's wisdom was greater than the wisdom of all the men of the East, and greater than all the wisdom of Egypt. He was wiser than any other man. . . . And his fame spread to all the surrounding nations. . . . Men of all nations came to listen to Solomon's wisdom. (1 Kings 4:29-34)

Why did those from neighboring lands want to hear what Solomon had to say? It was because he seemed to have found the key to what they all wanted—success.

King Solomon was greater in riches and wisdom than all the other kings of the earth. The whole world sought audience with Solomon to hear the wisdom God had put in his heart. (1 Kings 10:23-24)

Those who actually came to hear Solomon discovered something unique about his wisdom. Unlike the other powerful, wealthy kings of the region, Solomon did not take the credit for his achievements. In fact, he made a point of giving God the glory for all he had accomplished. He was doing it right. Basing his entire life upon relationship with the Almighty, Solomon submitted to the directives of divine revelation in order to use his creation endowment for good. As a result, people from pagan lands joined in worshiping the God of Israel.

> When the queen of Sheba saw all the wisdom of Solomon and the palace he had built, the food on his table, the seating of his officials, the attending servants in their robes, his cupbearers, and the burnt offerings he made at the temple of the Lord, she was overwhelmed. She said to the king, "The report I heard in my own country about your achievements and your wisdom is true. But I did not believe these things until I came and saw with my own eyes. Indeed, not even half was told me; in wisdom and wealth you have far exceeded the report I heard. How happy your men must be! How happy your officials, who continually stand before you and hear your wisdom! Praise be to the Lord your God, who has delighted in you and placed you on the throne of Israel. (1 Kings 10:4-9)

It all came together under the rule of Solomon. A group of fallen human beings submitted themselves to God's direction, used their abilities to build a civilization and culture to His glory, and became individually and corporately successful in the process. Enticed by the results, the pagan world was introduced to the God of Israel.

Similar situations happened throughout the Bible. Joseph had a major impact upon the ancient world by applying his exceptional wisdom in the role of vice pharaoh. Daniel and his friends were deported from their homeland to serve Babylon, yet they became the best and the brightest in that foreign land. Eventually their obedience led the king of Babylon himself to acknowledge the authority of the God of Israel. When the people of God live in submission to Him, great things happen!

THE BALANCE

We can go to one of two extremes in how we view ourselves. First, we can see ourselves as worthless and inept due to our fallen nature. When we live consistently with that view, we expect little from ourselves and accomplish nothing. Rather than glorifying God in this life, we just try to hold on until the life to come.

The other extreme is when we perceive ourselves to be the masters of our own destiny, able to achieve anything and everything we desire. When we live consistently with this view, we most likely accomplish a great deal and secure the praise of men. But in the process, we replace the directives of our Creator with our own selfish desires, which can lead to troublesome consequences.

The Bible outlines a balanced understanding of who we are, what we can accomplish, and what is the proper motivation for achievement. As beings created in God's image, we have infinite value and incredible abilities through our creation endowment. The intention has always been for us to use those abilities to glorify our Creator. Unfortunately, through the Fall, our objective has been altered. Now rather than seeking to glorify God through our accomplishments, we seek to glorify ourselves. The tragic effect of this shift is evident when we observe man's evil pursuits throughout history. In order to remedy this problem, three specific steps are necessary; relationship with God, revelation from God, and responsibility under God.

RELATIONSHIP WITH GOD

The overriding theme of the entire Bible is God's effort to reestablish relationship with His children. The Fall of man was a corporate rejection of God's authority, which can only be reversed on an individual basis. From the covenant with Abram to the crucifixion of God's own Son, the Lord has been reaching out His hand for us to hold as we cross the dangerous street of life. It is up to us to grab His hand and allow Him to lead the way.

Placing our trust in the provision made for our salvation through Jesus Christ is the beginning of a wonderful journey with God. We are not simply given the hope of eternal life at salvation. We are also given the opportunity to live with purpose and success through constant submission to the directives of our Lord.

REVELATION FROM GOD

Although the Fall did not eliminate our capacity for understanding and discovery, it did create a serious obstruction. As a result, we suppose that we are accurately perceiving the world and making wise decisions, but we are actually living out of step with reality. As one of my seminary professors explained, the fact that we are "tweeked" places us in need of divine direction.

God has provided the needed directives through the miracle of divine revelation. The Bible is an authoritative handbook on life. Without it, we have no absolute guide for correcting our misperceptions of truth. With it, we have the necessary guidance to more accurately understand the realities of life. As with a compass, its arrow will point us in the right direction, but we must choose to heed its guidance.

RESPONSIBILITY UNDER GOD

Once we have established a relationship with the Lord by submitting to His authority and countered our "tweek" by heeding His directives, we are ready to use our creation endowment for His glory. This is what responsible living is all about. We in the Christian community often end our message with points one and two. We preach salvation and obedience but seem to ignore the biblical emphasis on human achievement for the glory of God.

In a day when the achievements of mankind are reaching previously unparalleled heights, Christians seem to have settled into a retirement mode. Rather than striving to be at the forefront of societal change, we have retreated into a dangerously comfortable subculture. Whether because we think we can't compete with or ought not participate in the revolutionary changes around us, inactivity is an abdication of our God-given responsibility to affect society positively for Him.

BOTTOM LINE

The people of God are instructed both to declare and to demonstrate the truth through the way we live. Unfortunately, the message fails to communicate because those of us delivering it are just as messed up and irresponsible as those we are trying to convince. Consequently, we must properly understand our role and begin taking responsibility to affect society for His glory in a world bent on self-glorification.

5
Successful Living

*Men do less than they ought,
unless they do all that they can.*
Thomas Carlyle

As I discussed the issue of personal success with a pastor friend of mine he said, "I'd like to see my members become successful in their careers and leaders in the community, but how can I encourage them to do so when I worry that they will allow the trappings of success and power to corrupt them?"

My friend's question reflects a legitimate dilemma that all of us encounter at one time or another. We all have a deep desire to be successful and influential, but we aren't sure that it is right to seek such things. Unfortunately, this conflict is generally left unresolved, so capable Christians sit semi-idle while less gifted men and women with a godless worldview become the "movers and shakers" of society.

Most evangelicals are uncomfortable discussing the topic of success, let alone pursuing it. For some reason, we view poverty and insignificance as synonymous with godliness and humility. But, as can be observed from the biblical examples of Joseph, David, Solomon, Daniel, and others, God does not equate earthly success with heavenly failure. On the contrary, some of the most godly individuals in history have been highly prominent members of their societies.

Defining Success

Perhaps one reason we perceive a tension between Christian virtue and human ambition is our definition of success. Indeed, we do well to avoid following our culture's outline for prosperity and achievement. It requires beauty, wealth, power, and a healthy helping of ego. Let's face it, few of us will ever find our faces on the cover of *Forbes* or *Cosmopolitan.* Nor will we hear Robin Leach describing our lifestyle to the glassy-eyed masses in front of their television sets.

Real success has little to do with possessions or status. We need not step onto society's scale to weigh our level of merit. Rather than get caught up in a system that limits the definition of success to a temporal context, we should seek to be successful in all aspects of life.

I am not one to spiritualize commonly understood definitions. No matter how much we wrap it in religious jargon, the word *success* conjures up certain ideas for the average person. As typically used, being successful means reaching goals and attaining desired objectives, whether those objectives are financial security, professional status, harmonious relationships, or winning the World Series. No matter how you slice it, success must be understood in the context of achievement.

As we observed in chapter 4, God designed each of us with an incredible capacity for accomplishment, which we were to use to design, build, and maintain a civilization for the glorification of the Creator. Each individual would use his or her unique gifts to accomplish personal goals in the framework of divine objectives. Unfortunately, the Fall changed all that. We began playing with the loaded gun of human ability without the protective restraint of submission to God.

In His gracious wisdom, the Lord established a covenant with those willing to resubmit themselves to His plan. He offered relationship with Himself and revelation to help counter our damaged vision. Equipped with the necessary tools and direction, we are responsible to use the gifts He's given to impact society as His representatives. In this context, successful living means using our abilities to reach goals that are consistent with God's revealed will and dedicated to His glory. When we do so, we fulfill our responsibility to impact the world as His representatives.

Drawing upon these biblical themes, you can ask yourself several questions with regard to personal success. First, what specific gifts and abilities have you been given by God? Second, are you using those abilities to their fullest? Third, are your efforts dedicated to God's glory or your own gratification? Finally, in what ways does your life impact your world for good?

YOUR ENDOWMENT

You are an incredibly gifted person. You have been granted a combination of talents and abilities that no other person on the face of the earth can match. As a unique personality, you are able to relate to others in a style all your own. Your insights on life, drawn from your own experiences, are distinctive. In short, you are a one-of-a-kind masterpiece of God's creativity.

I have a very close friend named Dan. Dan and I attended the same church in Michigan during our high school years, became dorm roommates in California during college, and are now co-workers at Focus on the Family. We were friends through the trials of puberty, the turbulence of the dating years, the late nights of college cram sessions, the plunge of engagement, and the excitement of marriage. Our wives both gave birth to sons within a ten-day period, and we now force our boys to play with each other, hoping to make them into best buddies as well.

Needless to say, Dan has contributed a great deal to my life. He has encouraged me when I've needed a shot in the arm and challenged me when I've needed a kick in the pants. Our friendship has been one that reflects Solomon's proverb "As iron sharpens iron, so one man sharpens another" (Proverbs 27:17).

Despite our common experiences, Dan and I are radically different from one another in our interests, abilities, personalities, strengths, and weaknesses. Dan loves working with tools, I love working with ideas. Dan brings life to the party, I bring the food. Dan consoles those in crisis, I counsel them. Dan has struggled with self-worth, I have struggled with self-confidence. Both of us have wished we were like the other at one time or another.

By being just who God made him to be, however, Dan has added much to my life and to the lives of many others. His unique combination of gifts and abilities has contributed to my growth in ways he will never know. The reverse is also true. Certain aspects of my makeup that I consider insignificant have sharpened Dan's life. Both of us have learned through the years to appreciate our own giftedness, rather than continually wishing we were like the other. That lesson has been invaluable.

It is easy to covet the endowments of others so strongly that we totally ignore our own giftedness. There will always be someone who is stronger, faster, smarter, prettier, healthier, wealthier, and wittier to envy. But we cannot successfully use the gifts we have been given until we recognize and appreciate them. If you are like most people, feelings of low self-worth may blind you to the wonderful aspects of yourself that can be developed and used. Start the discovery process by recognizing the seemingly insignificant and common things. Make an intentional effort to identify the unique qualities you possess that can be used for good. Thank God for them, no matter how small or mundane they may seem. Remember, you are one of a kind, and no other person can fill your shoes.

YOUR EFFORT

When failure is inevitable, initiative is lost. If the desired objective cannot be obtained, why bother with the effort?

Our society has created an arbitrary standard of success that only the very attractive, rich, and powerful can attain. As a result, the average person perceives successful living as the lot of a privileged few. Since success is out of reach, he reasons, diligence is futile.

Fortunately, true success is within the reach of everyone, not just a lucky few. God's standard is not measured in terms of acquisition or status but in terms of faithfulness. Have you been responsible with the gifts and opportunities you've been given? If so, you are successful.

I have known many people who spend their lives watching others move upstream but never make an effort to do so themselves. They have the potential for significant achievement, but nothing is done with it. Whether defeated by the fear of failure or the comfort of complacency, they seem unwilling to grab the paddle and start rowing.

When defined in relation to individual ability, successful living means holding yourself accountable to give one hundred percent to the task of life. It means developing your abilities rather than developing excuses. It means going as far as possible with the opportunities before you rather than settling for the status quo. Anything less is an irresponsible use of your God-given gifts.

YOUR MOTIVATION

Once upon a time, a group of people got together to build a great tower. It was designed to reach into the heavens and as a gathering point for worship. As the magnificent tower neared completion, God intervened and stopped their progress. He was severely displeased with their efforts and would not allow them to finish their task.

Much later, in another land, a different group of people began building a similar structure. This building was also designed as a gathering point for men and women to worship. But the Lord did not stop them from finishing their temple. In fact, upon completion, He personally indwelt one of its rooms. He was pleased with their efforts and blessed them for their diligence.

What was the difference between these two projects? After all, both were meant to be places of worship. Both involved long, difficult hours of labor on the part of thousands of people. Both were designed and crafted with the highest attention to detail and beauty. Why were the outcomes so radically different?

The answer becomes clear when you look at the context of each example. The first was the ancient tower of Babel, which was being built to glorify man. The second was Solomon's Temple, which was built as a place to worship God. Although the levels of diligence were identical, the sources of motivation were directly opposite.

When the motive of any endeavor is self-adulation, whether it is conscious or not, our natural pull toward evil will corrupt our efforts. Building a tower was a perfectly acceptable task for the people of Babel to attempt. The problem was not in the task but in the objective. They wanted a focal point of the city that would remind them of their own greatness. "Then they said, 'Come, let us build ourselves a city, with a tower that reaches to the heavens, so that we may make a name for ourselves and not be scattered over the face of the whole earth'" (Genesis 11:4).

By contrast, the people of Israel built the Temple as a continual point of remembrance to the greatness of their God.

> Then the king and all Israel with him offered sacrifices before the Lord. . . . So the king and all the Israelites dedicated the temple of the Lord. . . . On the following day he sent the people away. They blessed the king and then went home, joyful and glad in heart for all the good things the Lord had done for his servant David and his people Israel. (1 Kings 8:62-66)

I began this chapter with my friend's concern regarding the dangers of pursuing success and influence. I believe that proper motivation is the key to avoiding the pitfalls commonly allied with achievement. If self-gratification is my motivation, then the end justifies the means and everything is negotiable. If bringing glory to God is truly the driving force behind all of my efforts, I will live in continual submission to His revealed moral will.

Thus, it is imperative that we continually check our motives. Ask yourself on a daily basis whether your efforts are dedicated to God's glory or your own. True success demands no less.

YOUR IMPACT

Every individual has some effect upon society, whether for good or for bad. In ways that are great or small, public or private, intentional or accidental, all of us touch the lives of others. The wealthy corporate executive and the impoverished single mother share the same mission, though different in scope. Each is responsible for his or her sphere of influence.

You may find yourself in a nine-to-five factory job. Or you may have the responsibility to oversee million-dollar engineering projects. Either way, true success is measured by the same criteria: how you handle the opportunities specific to your situation.

Are you married? If so, how do your words and actions impact your mate? If you are a parent, do you make an intentional effort to influence the lives of your children for good? When you are at work, do you give your best effort when no one else will notice? Are you a responsible citizen willing to obey the laws of the land, even at tax time? Do you support your local church, give to the poor, care for the sick, vote, and pay your bills? All of those common actions contribute to your impact on society.

If part of God's plan for your life is to influence society as His representative, an honest evaluation of your impact is essential. You are impacting the lives of others for good or for bad.

Too often we consider the mundane aspects of life insignificant. But truly successful people try never to forget that it is in the routine and daily that we have our greatest influence upon others.

True success is measured not by our level of achievement but by our level of responsibility. Using this definition, each of us is equally able to be successful. At the same time, each of us is equally able to fail.

The person with little ability who is responsible with his opportunities is far more successful than the celebrated individual who relies upon talent rather than effort. In other words, a genius who casually earns an A minus is a failure compared to the imbecile who labors to earn a C plus. This principle was clearly stated by Jesus when He said, "From everyone who has been given much, much will be demanded; and from the one who has been entrusted with much, much more will be asked" (Luke 12:48*b*).

When we are responsible with the gifts we've been given and our efforts are dedicated to God's glory, we will have a positive influence upon our world. Under normal circumstances, our positive influence upon others will indirectly reap personal benefits. There is no need to be apologetic or embarrassed when blessings come. Healthy relationships, financial freedom, professional excellence, and other upstream ambitions are an indirect outcome when your primary objective is responsible living.

AMBUSHED BY SUCCESS

The accomplishment of goals and the acquisition of things will prompt one of two attitudes: pride in yourself or praise to your God. Success is positive. But with it comes the need to actively avoid the deception its benefits can bring.

It is somewhat perplexing to observe the typical pattern of success. When times are lean, we seek God's hand of provision. Once that provision comes, however, we quickly forget its source. We convince ourselves that our own efforts are the sole reason for our good fortune. Sadly, it often requires another slice of difficulty to bring us back to our senses.

To avoid being ambushed by success, we must maintain a proper perspective when the good times come by remembering the true source of life and blessing.

MASTER OF YOUR DESTINY

We live in the "me" generation. The pursuit of personal gratification is seen as an essential ingredient of civilized life. Self-denial is the stuff of medieval monasteries, not twentieth-century culture. The truly successful person, so our society says, is the one who takes charge of his own fate and becomes master of his own destiny.

Despite our culture's emphasis on self-glorification, it is imperative that we pursue personal goals in light of biblical teaching. We are *not* the masters of our own destinies! Every breath we take is a gift from the Almighty, and He can take it away as easily as He gives it. The moment we lose sight of our utter dependence upon God, we cross the line into self-deception. Only He knows where the steps we take today will carry us tomorrow. We must walk continually recognizing that the Lord is the true master of our destinies. "In his heart a man plans his course, but the Lord determines his steps" (Proverbs 16:9).

Although we may not be in total control of the direction of our lives, we are responsible for our own choices, beliefs, and actions. Herein lies the balance. God grants us the freedom to choose our path, holding us responsible for the choices we make. At the same time, we can walk in confidence, knowing that He is able to weave our frail efforts into a splendid tapestry of success.

BOTTOM LINE

When pursuing personal success, consider these important questions. What specific gifts and abilities has God given you? Are you using those abilities to their fullest? Are your efforts dedicated to God's glory or your own gratification? And how does your life impact your world for good?

Section Three
THE PADDLE PRINCIPLES

*Before we can consistently row upstream,
we must understand the broad life principles
that enable us to replace victimization
with personal responsibility.*

6
The Necessity of Truth

Men occasionally stumble over the truth,
but most of them pick themselves up
and hurry off as if nothing happened.
Winston Churchill

Nearly every suburban neighborhood has one dog that strikes terror in the heart of every little kid. My block was no exception. The dog was Rasha. Though my buddies and I were ordinary five-year-old boys, Rasha was no ordinary dog.

Rasha was a Great Dane that looked more like a small horse than a large dog. All of us were convinced that he could leap over the fence whenever he pleased. Needless to say, we avoided his yard and lived in fearful anticipation of the day Rasha would escape and seek young, tender children as an afternoon snack.

One day, to everyone's terror, it happened. One of the neighborhood kids screamed, "Rasha's loose! Run for your lives!" No quicker were the words out of his mouth than every kid on the block scattered to the nearest available shelter. In less than five seconds, a street full of children at play became empty and lifeless. It was a matter of hours before the first brave soul dared to set foot outside, only to discover that it had been a false alarm. Rasha had been napping the whole time.

What we believe to be true has a direct impact upon our behavior, regardless of whether that belief is consistent with reality. Rasha posed no actual threat to the neighborhood kids, but our panic was genuine nonetheless. Had we investigated the accuracy of the warning before acting upon it, our reaction would have been quite different. By accepting as fact that which was actually a lie, we chose the wrong course of action.

Such is the pattern of life. We live consistent with what we believe to be true, even when we are mistaken. The more our understanding of the world conforms to reality, the better our choices will be. The more we operate under false assumptions, the worse our judgment becomes.

LIFE MAP

Few things are as frustrating as the effort to locate a new address using a less than precise map. My wife tends to trust her memory when listening to directions, usually missing certain details. In contrast, I typically ask probing questions about distances between streets and landmarks, using crayons and a ruler to draw a map that will be color coded and to scale. The diagram in hand when we pull out of the driveway generally ends up somewhere in between these two extremes.

We have arrived at many social gatherings late and tense as a result of our combined mapping efforts. We either miss the right street, turn onto the wrong one, or drive the wrong direction down the right street. Once in the general area, we circle the block several times before stopping at a pay phone to call. It can be embarrassing.

Just as a reliable map is essential for getting to an unfamiliar location, our understanding of the world must be accurate if we hope to attain our objectives in life. Imagine the frustration and futility of trying to find an address in Denver using a map of Dallas. Yet, we often make important life decisions based upon a faulty worldview, and the consequences can be far worse than simple embarrassment.

Each of us develops his or her life map according to various factors. As children, we began to understand the world from the instruction and example of our parents. As we grow, teachers and peer relationships make their own unique contributions to our developing map. As adults, exposure to the universe of ideas and belief patterns solidifies our worldview. The input we receive from each of those sources has significant impact upon our overall life map, for better or worse.

If life is generally difficult but my map says it should be easy, I will encounter disillusionment. My belief about life will not change reality. It will, however, cause me to have expectations and make decisions that are inconsistent with what is true. I will make wrong turns on a regular basis.

Those who follow the wrong map may become frustrated by the inefficiency of their efforts. Other people seem to make much more progress than they do, somehow reaching their goals with far less exertion. They may fail to understand that advancement is not determined by the amount of energy we expend but by whether or not we are heading in the right direction.

The first requirement of personal responsibility is a simple commitment to developing a life map that is consistent with reality. We must be willing to replace false views with truth. When we discover behavior patterns that grow out of faulty understanding, we must take the steps necessary to practice what is right. Truth is an absolute necessity if we hope to reach our upstream objectives.

FICTIONAL TRUTH

It seems elementary to suggest that living a life that is consistent with reality is the first step toward responsibility. However, several factors complicate what should be a simple process. Distinguishing the truth from a lie can be difficult, especially when the lie is perceived as the truth.

The best movies are those that pull your emotions into the story as if you were personally involved with the drama. You feel the pain and joy of the characters just as intensely as you would in real life. Fine art encourages you to perceive fiction as truth.

Throughout the drama of life we can create fictional truths. When we believe that false perceptions are true, we respond to them accordingly. Some adults, for example, struggle with their family life due to fictional truths they learned growing up. Their only point of reference for understanding relationships came from a dysfunctional situation, which colored their expectation of how things are supposed to be.

Others may find it difficult to believe certain objective truths due to seemingly contradictory experience. Maria's situation as described in chapter 1 is a case in point. Although she wanted to embrace a God who loved her, the trauma of her sexual abuse seemed to suggest that He didn't. After all, if He loved her, shouldn't He have protected her?

The answer is to replace lies with the truth. Until we are able to do that, we will continue to see life through our fictional perceptions. But discerning the truth is not accomplished overnight.

Wrong Directions

All of us, to one degree or another, have an imperfect life map. The points of deviation must be identified and corrected as soon as possible. Unfortunately, our tendency as fallen people is to reject what is true in favor of what is comfortable and to choose what is familiar over what is right. As painful as fiction may be, it is often preferred over reality. As Jesus stated, "And this is the condemnation, that light is come into the world, and men loved darkness rather than light, because their deeds were evil" (John 3:19, KJV*).

We don't admit openly that we wish to remain in darkness rather than be confronted with the light. Our self-deception is more subtle. We disguise our rejection of the truth by couching it in terms of acceptance and open-mindedness. Our maps remain flawed nonetheless.

TRUTH IS RELATIVE

In his number one best-selling book, *The Closing of the American Mind,* Allan Bloom provides commentary on the generally accepted premise of our culture.

> There is one thing a professor can be absolutely certain of: almost every student entering the university believes, or says he believes, that truth is relative. If this belief is put to the test, one can count on the students' reaction: they will be uncomprehending. That anyone should regard the proposition as non self-evident astonishes them, as though he were calling into question $2 + 2 = 4$. . . . The danger they have been taught to fear from absolutism is not error but intolerance. . . . Openness—and the relativism that makes it the only plausible stance in the face of various claims to truth and various ways of life and kinds of human beings—is the great insight of our times. The true believer is

*King James Version.

the real danger. . . . *The point is not to correct the mistakes and really be right; rather it is not to think you are right at all.*[1] (Italics added)

Dialogue and debate about what is true have diminished due to the relativity that Bloom describes. Rather than looking up for understanding, we look within. We are encouraged to become our own source of truth and our own god.

I believe that one of the reasons New Age religions have been sweeping Western society is this cultural longing to discard absolute truth. Why are discerning individuals willing to accept a worldview that actively discourages rational thought? Because rational thought leads to claims of truth, which in turn must be accepted or rejected. Mystical contemplation, on the other hand, respects only individual experience. The task of accepting and rejecting facts is eliminated, and "harmony" is attained.

Some time ago the Associated Press released a story about E. Frenkel, one of the Soviet Union's increasing number of psychics. He claimed that he had successfully used his extraordinary abilities to stop bicycles, automobiles, and streetcars. His next trick would be to stop a freight train. Frenkel stepped onto the tracks to face the oncoming train, confident that his psychic-biological powers would force it to stop. They didn't, and it didn't, and he was killed instantly. In the reality created by E. Frenkel, the train stopped. In the reality created by God, it didn't.

No matter how strongly we believe that our view of truth is right, if it is inconsistent with reality, it isn't! The law of gravity is just as tough on the guy who thinks he can fly as it is on the rest of us.

Although each of us must *discover* truth for ourselves, that does not mean that we should *create* our own truth. Rather than holding the data suspect when people interpret it differently, we should question the competence of those doing the interpreting. Absolute truth does exist, despite the fact that none of us has perfect understanding. Remember, our vision is damaged due to the Fall.

PICK AND CHOOSE

There are many things that are true that I hate. Certain physical realities, such as pain and death, are extremely unpleasant.

There are many spiritual truths that I don't like to acknowledge, such as human depravity and divine judgment. I'd like to eliminate their existence through disbelief, but I can't. When I refuse to accept their reality, I only deceive myself.

Those of us within the evangelical community can convince ourselves that we always accept the truth. After all, we pride ourselves on having the right answers. But we are not really different from unbelievers in this area. What we hear is often dictated by what we *want* to hear. We subtly reject those truths which seem unattractive in favor of those we find palatable.

We tend to treat truths like a rack of clothes in the shopping mall. We sort through them one at a time, selecting those we like, bypassing those we don't. God's grace fits our taste, but His justice doesn't. Human potential looks appealing, but not human depravity. By the time we're finished, reality is distorted at best and absent at worst.

The apostle Paul spoke of the tendency to accept only those things which seem pleasant.

> For the time will come when men will not put up with sound doctrine. Instead, to suit their own desires, they will gather around them a great number of teachers to say what their itching ears want to hear. They will turn their ears away from the truth and turn aside to myths. (2 Timothy 4:3-4)

By emphasizing those truths that are attractive to the exclusion of those that seem more harsh, we actually reject reality. As the saying goes, truth out of balance is error. When we begin to listen to and accept only those things that "tickle the ears," we end up drafting a map that is appealing but virtually useless.

FOOLISH BLISS

Discovering the truth is no easy task. There are so many religious, philosophical, and theoretical perspectives on the fundamental issues of life that it boggles the mind. How does one investigate all alternatives, let alone choose one over the rest? Due to the difficulty of the assignment, many of us don't even bother with it. After all, ignorance is bliss!

Certainly, many tough questions will never be answered in this life. In fact, the theme of the book of Job is that life doesn't always make sense and that certain issues will remain unresolved. But Job also teaches that God has everything under control and that we must depend upon His guidance when we don't understand. He has revealed enough through natural revelation (creation) and special revelation (the Bible) to guide us through this life. He will explain the rest when we get home.

Intellectual assent to the existence of absolute truth is one thing; working to understand it is altogether different. Many evangelical Christians demand a doctrinal statement that upholds scriptural authority, while they neglect personal investigation and application of the Bible in their own lives. It is easy to sign a statement of belief, but it takes work to personally discover and live the truth.

My undergraduate years were spent at a small Christian college. I was one of those students who tended to question everything taught, to the delight of some professors and the frustration of others. I perceived academic training as an opportunity to actively investigate rather than as a passive process of indoctrination. Not all of my classmates shared that perspective.

On one occasion a fellow student intercepted me near my dorm and asked me a disturbing question after a doctrinal discussion in class. "Kurt, what do we believe about . . . ?"

Now, I don't mind being asked my viewpoint on a given subject, and I enjoy dialogue on controversial topics as much as anyone. But it caught me off guard to be asked, "What do *we* believe?" I responded by asking, "I don't know. What *do* you believe?" His responsibility was to investigate the options and arrive at a conclusion, not parrot someone else's position.

We can become so dependent upon the reasoning of others that we never bother to think for ourselves. Although we may end up with the right position, we learn nothing in the process. It is perfectly appropriate to seek the guidance of others and look to gifted teachers for instruction. However, those steps are intended to enhance personal discovery, not replace it.

It is distressing to observe the number of people who refuse to think for themselves. Hooked on formulas for living taught by their favorite celebrity mentors, they lose their ability to make independent decisions. Due to shallow understanding, they fear taking any course of action without a stamp of approval from the teacher.

God has granted every one of us the ability to think for himself. We are expected to use the minds we have been given to discover what is true and live consistently with reality. When we neglect to do so, irresponsibility is inevitable.

Through a Glass Darkly

Part of understanding the truth is recognizing the limits of our comprehension. Although it is foolish to claim that knowing any truth is impossible, it is equally absurd to think that we know all truth. Both extremes drive us to irresponsible decisions and perspectives.

Many people have difficulty accepting certain truths because they are unable to understand how or why they are so. But we are not always given the answer to such questions. We must be willing to accept what God has revealed as true, whether or not all of our questions are resolved.

If I were to ask you to explain how a tiny seed becomes a mighty tree, could you? Most would describe the process of planting the seed in the soil, watering it, and watching its eventual breaking through the ground into the sunlight. But they would be describing *what* happens, not *how* it happens. Few can explain how the chemical exchange process works or how the roots know when and where to grow. Yet despite our inability to explain the hows, few of us would consider it foolish to believe that planted seeds become mighty trees. We accept the *what*, with little to no idea how or why.

The balance in understanding truth is distinguishing between the whats and the hows. God has revealed many of the whats in life, such as His character and our need. But He has chosen not to reveal many of the hows and whys that haunt us. Instead, He asks us to take His hand and trust Him. That is what the life of faith is all about. It is believing what has been revealed, living consistently with its reality, and trusting that God has the larger scheme of things in hand.

When we claim to have perfect understanding, we only deceive ourselves. On the other hand, when we claim an inability to know *anything,* we shirk our responsibility to learn. We cannot allow the mysteries of life to prevent our knowledge of the clearly revealed. God has provided the capacity and information necessary to draw a reliable map. He has left the task of doing it up to us.

DRAWING THE RIGHT MAP

As we have seen, our worldview has a significant impact upon our actions, and when it is faulty we live inconsistently with reality. Responsible living requires commitment to several principles for drawing an accurate life map. First, we must be willing to discover the truth, regardless of the discipline it takes. Second, it is essential that we accept what is true, no matter how unpleasant it may be. Finally, once we determine and accept the truth, we must begin the process of living consistently with reality.

NO MATTER HOW DIFFICULT—DISCOVER IT

There are some relatively simple means for investigating and discovering truth. One of the primary reasons for weekly church attendance, for example, is to receive regular instruction from the Word of God. The more we understand His special revelation to us, the better we are able to interpret the data of life. As the only authoritative source of truth, the Scriptures are the most vital link in the chain of comprehension.

As beneficial as it is to sit under biblical instruction, however, discovering the truth is more than passively receiving information. We must also actively investigate the dynamics that make up our unique perspective. Past and present influences may color the lenses through which we observe the world. Examining those influences can be difficult, even painful.

The currents of past experience can be some of the toughest issues to face when attempting to redraw a life map that is consistent with reality. Revisiting memories that we have successfully suppressed for years is a painful process, often requiring the guidance and support of a trained counselor or trusted friend. By doing so, however, we are able to identify sources of confusion and misinformation in our lives.

In chapter 1, I introduced Janice, who struggled with her identity in the context of repeated rejection in her youth. Once she recognizes the hindrance to her healthy self-image, she will be able to replace the lie of inadequacy with the truth of infinite worth. If, on the other hand, she remains in the "comfort" zone of self-defeat, she will continue to follow a life map based upon faulty data.

Maria was sexually abused by her dad. She must place the responsibility for that evil on her father where it belongs, rather than taking it upon herself or placing it on God. How can she relate to God as a loving Father while her family's secret clouds her perception of reality?

Realizing the truth about our own blind spots can also be painful. None of us is perfect, but we like to think we are closer than the next guy. It is tough to accept revelation of offensive personal habits or improper attitudes. Our immediate reaction is to become defensive or to excuse our actions. By using such occasions as an opportunity to discover further insights about our life map, however, we can avoid repeating the same wrong behavior over and over again.

We must commit ourselves to discovering the truth about the world around us as well as our own misperceptions and weaknesses. Even when the process is difficult, the benefits far outweigh the cost.

NO MATTER HOW UNPLEASANT—ACCEPT IT

During the early reign of Adolf Hitler, discussion over how to respond to the popular leader of the German people was heated among the political leaders of Europe. Some saw him as a serious threat who should not be trusted. Others held a less cautious view, confident that his gains in political influence and military strength were a petty concern. The newly installed Prime Minister of England, Neville Chamberlain, simply wanted to keep the German issue in proper perspective. He had many ambitious goals for his country and didn't want alarmists such as Winston Churchill stirring up unwarranted anxiety among the people.

Chamberlain was not the only member of the government with a less than positive attitude toward Churchill. Most in Parliament found his frequent speeches about the rising threat of Hitler bothersome. The progressive goals of the Chamberlain administration were far more appealing than the doom and gloom ramblings of an old man. Undaunted by the apathy of his colleagues, however, Churchill continued sounding the alarm of advances in German military capability and the need to prepare for an eventual war. World War II was knocking at the door, but most ignored that unpleasant reality. Consequently, England entered the war ill-equipped to counter the tremendous power of the Third Reich.

Our criticism of the English Parliament for discounting Churchill's warnings should be mellowed by the realization that we possess the same inclination toward self-deception. Their "see no evil" response to the truth illustrates our own tendency to reject those realities that are unpleasant. When the truth is unappealing, we typically avoid it and sometimes deny its existence altogether.

Many refuse to accept the reality of a personal God because they are unwilling to submit to His authority. Although they claim to reject God's existence on intellectual grounds, the real issue is more volitional than rational. Some of the greatest thinkers in the modern world have demonstrated that the evidence of God's existence is compelling. Yet those who desire autonomy refuse to examine it for fear they will be forced to acknowledge the "unpleasant" reality of a sovereign God.

Those who become entangled in unhealthy relationships often resist acknowledging the harmful realities of co-dependence or of enabling self-destructive behavior. They may know subconsciously that admitting their unhealthy tendencies will require eventual change. Since change is uncomfortable, they choose instead to continue a cycle of relational immaturity and defeat. Truth is rejected in order to maintain the status quo.

Regardless of how unpleasant it may be, we must be willing to accept the truth. The realities of life will impact us just as forcefully if we deny them as if we accept them. By accepting them, however, we are better equipped to deal with the bad things and enjoy the good things. When we live in denial, we set ourselves up for certain disillusionment and potential calamity.

NO MATTER HOW INCONVENIENT—LIVE IT

After we have identified and accepted the truth, we must also begin living consistently with reality. What is the point of having an accurate map when we keep referring to the faulty one? We are in Denver, so let's stop using the Dallas map!

It is not always easy to live consistently with what is true, especially when others insist upon maintaining the lies of a fallen world. Those who live the lies typically resist those who live the truth. Confrontation with reality can be unsettling. Therefore, we must anticipate resistance when we try to do right in a world gone wrong.

Relationships can be strained when we stop allowing others to perpetuate destructive behavior. Professional advancement can be hindered when we refuse to compromise principle. Personal comfort can be sacrificed when we begin the process of personal growth. But we should expect no less from those who remain committed to the lies of a fallen world. As Jesus said, "If the world hates you, keep in mind that it hated me first" (John 15:18).

Not only does living consistently with the truth create resistance from others, it can cause tension within ourselves. If I have believed myself to be worthless and unloved from childhood, it will not be easy to change my actions and reactions to match the truth that God loves me and created me with infinite worth. It will require a long process of redrawing my map and relearning how I will live.

> Do not conform any longer to the pattern of this world, but be transformed by the renewing of your mind. Then you will be able to test and approve what God's will is—his good, pleasing and perfect will. (Romans 12:2)

Again, we will live according to what we believe to be true, whether that belief is valid or not. Transforming the mind is a lifelong process of replacing false beliefs with true ones. The more accurately our beliefs line up with reality, the more accurate our attitudes and actions will be.

FREEDOM

We live in a society that considers the idea of absolute truth unacceptable, even dangerous. The true believer is the only real hindrance to the goal of utopia. The message comes across loud and clear: remove the "dangers" of religious conviction and absolutism, and the world will finally experience peaceful coexistence.

The desire for world unity and global harmony is commendable. However, living a fantasy will not accomplish that goal. By abandoning the idea of truth, we do not gain freedom from the evils of the world; we are blinded to their inevitability. According to Jesus, it is truth itself that frees us. "You will know the truth, and the truth will set you free" (John 8:32).

Following an accurate map on the journey of life does not restrict us; it frees us. True freedom doesn't come from aimless wandering. It comes from knowing where we are, where we are going, and how to get there.

BOTTOM LINE

We live consistently with what we believe to be true, whether or not our beliefs are accurate. The first requirement of personal responsibility is a commitment to developing a life map that matches up with reality. We must be willing to discover, accept, and live the truth, regardless of how difficult or unpleasant it may be.

7
The Impact of Choices

He who chooses the beginning of a road
chooses the place it leads to.
It is the means that determine the end.
Harry Emerson Fosdick

Our society highly values the freedom of choice. We can decide where we will reside, what we will do for a living, and how or whether we will worship God. Our Founding Fathers recognized that such choices should be left to the individual citizen rather than the ruling class. With the exception of certain laws, which are designed to maintain order and protect rights, we have unrestricted freedom to choose our own direction in life.

Of course, the concept of free choice was not original with those who formed our early government. God Himself created man with the ability and freedom to make his own decisions. We are not robots forced to conform to God's every wish. Desiring relationship based on free choice, God designed us in such a way that we are able to determine our own actions and attitudes. The freedom to choose is a precious aspect of who we are as created in the image of God.

Unfortunately, the choices we make are not always in line with what is best. Ever since the Fall, our disposition toward harmful choices has turned this wonderfully unique feature of human existence into our most self-destructive quality. God gave us the freedom to choose with one major stipulation—that we accept responsibility for the outcome. The flip side to choice is consequence.

Although our culture loves its right to choose, it reacts in violent protest against any suggestion that we suffer repercussions for our harmful choices. God does not remove the freedom to choose, even when we misuse it. Neither will He remove the consequences, even when we ignore them.

The impact of daily choices cannot be overstated. The law of sowing and reaping is as real as the law of gravity. When we make wise decisions, we reap positive results. When we choose the way of the fool, we reap folly.

CONSEQUENCES

The Old Testament narrative describes a constant cycle of choice and consequence for the people of God. When they chose to live in obedience to God's covenant, they were blessed and successful. When they chose to follow other gods and live in disobedience, they encountered serious adversity. Their immoral and foolish choices brought destructive results upon them. God used divine discipline to compel those living in error to come back home.

The example of Israel illustrates a principle that directly impacts individuals today: Wrong choices lead to harmful consequences. The book of Proverbs is a gallery of representations of this reality:

> The evil deeds of a wicked man ensnare him; the cords of his sin hold him fast. He will die for lack of discipline, led astray by his own great folly. (Proverbs 5:22-23)
> Diligent hands will rule, but laziness ends in slave labor. (Proverbs 12:24)
> A quick-tempered man does foolish things, and a crafty man is hated. (Proverbs 14:17)
> A man who remains stiff-necked after many rebukes will suddenly be destroyed—without remedy. (Proverbs 29:1)

As one reads through the book of Proverbs it becomes apparent that the primary difference between the fool and the wise man is the way they make decisions. The fool tends to be impulsive, living for the moment without considering the long-range impact of his choices. The wise man, on the other hand, gives careful thought to how today's actions will impact tomorrow.

"A prudent man sees danger and takes refuge, but the simple keep going and suffer for it" (Proverbs 22:3).

THE ANT

Ants are amazing little creatures. If you've ever observed them for longer than it takes to squash one underfoot, you know that they are incredibly strong. How many times have you seen a tiny black ant carrying an object far larger than itself, often for long distances, such as from your picnic basket to its mound across the park? It would seem that more than any other qualities, strength and endurance would place the ant on the honorable mention list for "most likely to succeed" pests. Yet it is another trait altogether for which the ant is mentioned in the writings of Solomon.

Unlike other insects that live for the moment, the ant plans for the rainy day. As Solomon explains, "Go to the ant, you sluggard; consider its ways and be wise! It has no commander, no overseer or ruler, yet it stores its provisions in summer and gathers its food at harvest" (Proverbs 6:6-8).

That the typical ant pulls out his handy dandy, year-at-a-glance pocket calendar every morning to check out the day's scheduled activities is unlikely. After all, how many alternatives does an ant have? It's either gather food or sit around waiting to be squashed by those insensitive two-leggers.

But Solomon's point is well-taken. Ants instinctively do what we slightly more sophisticated creatures tend to neglect: evaluate the long-range impact of today's activities. Rather than coast through life with nary a care waiting for someone else to assign the responsibilities, they hold themselves accountable to do what needs to be done.

All too often we make decisions without serious forethought regarding the long-range consequences. We throw up a quick prayer for wisdom (the Christian version of crossing one's fingers) and proceed to choose the easiest option before us. Then, when things fall apart, we blame God for failing to answer our prayer. But in reality *we* made the unwise and hasty choice.

Just as the ant plans for tomorrow on his own, we must take individual responsibility to evaluate the impact of our own choices and actions. After all, like it or not, we must suffer the consequences for the results. Rather than look to others to lead us to do what's right, we should take it upon ourselves to live a wise and responsible lifestyle. Most of our big mistakes are due to lack of forethought rather than intentional misdoings.

There are consequences to every choice we make, good or bad. Once we accept that principle, we can make it work for us rather than against us. We must consider the impact of today's actions and attitudes on the future, then choose those things that will bring long-range benefit rather than short-range gratification.

THE PRODIGAL

We tend to think that God is obliged to protect us from harm, even when we live like fools, simply because we are His children. But He sometimes allows us to suffer the consequences of our actions in order to bring us to our senses, as Jesus illustrated through His story of the prodigal son.

> There was a man who had two sons. The younger one said to his father, "Father, give me my share of the estate." So he divided his property between them. Not long after that, the younger son got together all he had, set off for a distant country and there squandered his wealth in wild living. (Luke 15:11-13)

Notice that the father, who represents God in this story, did not try to prevent his son from making a foolish choice. He granted him the freedom to decide his own course in life, even though that meant squandering away his entire fortune. As we will see, the father also allowed him to suffer the consequences of his actions and learn from his error.

> After he had spent everything, there was a severe famine in that whole country, and he began to be in need. So he went and hired himself out to a citizen of that country, who sent him to his fields to feed pigs. He longed to fill his stomach with the pods that the pigs were eating, but no one gave him anything. (Luke 15:14-16)

It is no small thing for a Jew to end up feeding pigs, an animal considered most unclean. At this point the father could have sent out servants to check on his beloved son. After all, there was a famine in the land, and the father must have worried about his boy. Still, he allowed the son to endure the outcome of foolish living, even to the point of humility and hunger. As a result, the boy came to his senses.

> When he came to his senses, he said, "How many of my father's hired men have food to spare, and here I am starving to death! I will set out and go back to my father and say to him: Father, I have sinned against heaven and against you. I am no longer worthy to be called your son; make me like one of your hired men." (Luke 15:17-19)

The son did not have a deep, spiritual experience that revealed to him the error of his ways. He simply got hungry enough to stop and consider what an idiot he had been! Because he was willing to accept responsibility for his foolish choices, he was able to understand the impact they had upon his life. As a result, the story ends with a family reunion and the boy getting his life back on track.

Consider what the outcome might have been had the boy refused to accept his responsibility. What if he had blamed God for abandoning him in his time of need when the hunger pangs came? What if he had blamed his inability to get a better job on poor social policy? What if he had charged his father with parental neglect for giving him all that money before he was ready to handle it properly? In so doing, he would have made himself a victim in order to avoid taking personal responsibility for his actions.

We often derive a perverse sense of satisfaction from feeling sorry for ourselves in our failure and discontent. Assuming the world owes us something, we bemoan the "bum rap" handed to us by our uncaring church, insensitive family, inept employer, or even unfair God. Yet, every one of us has made our own choices. If we wallow as victims, we will be unable to overcome our destructive tendencies. Not until we understand that we are part of the problem can we become part of the solution.

VICTIMS BY CHOICE

Imagine sitting in the corner of a doctor's office listening to his consultations for a day. During the day, two cases with the same diagnosis are discussed. But they are drastically different. In case number one, Bill has contracted a terminal illness, and he has less than one year to live. The second case involves John, who also is given twelve months to live. John's problem, however, is not a deadly disease but his lifestyle. For years John has been eating poorly, neglecting physical exercise, smoking heavily, and suffering severe stress in his job. As a result, the doctor says, he is a prime candidate for a heart attack.

The doctor is completely honest with Bill, advising him to update his will and prepare for his death. On the other hand, he offers John hope. Because John's problems are the result of poor habits, he could improve his health by altering his lifestyle. If he quits smoking, adopts a healthy diet, begins a regular exercise program, and slows down at work, he could live many more years. If he changes nothing, however, John's death is as certain as Bill's.

John can choose one of two reactions. He can accept the doctor's advice to begin living in a more healthy manner, or he can become upset with the doctor for making him feel guilty about his lifestyle. "How can you be so insensitive?" he may ask. "It's bad enough telling me that I'm going to die. You don't have to make me feel worse by blaming me too! How can you point accusing fingers at a time like this? I'm a dying man!"

As foolish as that reaction sounds, it reflects an all too common perspective toward life's difficulties. Faced with the prospect of acknowledging personal error, we choose instead to see ourselves as victims. Consequently, we throw away hope for recovery. Hope comes only when we are part of the problem. If I am indeed a victim of uncontrollable agents, changing myself will accomplish nothing. If, on the other hand, I am part of the problem, I can also be part of the solution.

HEALING

Over the past several years the Christian community has been deluged by books and seminars on the need for healing—of childhood memories, relationships, addictions, inner struggles, and so on. This trend has increased general awareness of the need to deal with unresolved issues in life. Using the *healing* word picture, however, has also created some misunderstandings.

The word *healing* suggests passive waiting rather than active participation in recovery. When considering their need for "healing," many picture themselves lying in a hospital bed, passively allowing a wound to mend or a symptom to disappear. Consequently, those who really need to confront certain currents instead wait passively for the Lord or time to "heal" their hurt.

Perhaps a more appropriate example is the process of rehabilitation after an injury. If you've ever broken a leg, you know that the time of inactive healing is relatively short. The actual rehabilitation, on the other hand, can take quite some time. In the beginning, you take short steps with the assistance of a cane or crutch. Then by standing and limping you begin to strengthen the weakened leg. After intense discipline and frequent confrontation of the pain, you eventually regain full use of the injured limb.

REHABILITATION

A friend of mine who works in physical rehabilitation observed that not everyone enters into treatment with the same motivation or desire for recovery. Even when two patients have identical injuries, the time it takes for one to regain full strength can be significantly longer than for the other. The difference lies in what each has at stake.

If a professional athlete suffers a debilitating leg injury during practice, he takes personal responsibility for his recovery. Since his livelihood is at stake, he endures the necessary pain to get his leg back in shape. The primary concern on the part of those working with him is not that he will become apathetic but that he will try to progress too quickly.

On the other hand, those who think they have something to gain from remaining incapacitated take much longer to recover. Perhaps a personal injury lawsuit is pending, and they hope to increase the settlement. Maybe their suffering gets them extra attention or special treatment at home. Perceived benefits of the injury may decrease the motivation necessary for a full recovery.

This principle holds true beyond the physical realm. Those who believe they have something to gain by remaining victims of past experience, present circumstance, or other people will refuse to accept personal responsibility for their own advancement. As a result, their recovery is prolonged, if not averted altogether.

IT HURTS TOO MUCH

Cindy was abused as a child, and everyone knows it. Every time the minister asks for prayer requests, Cindy's hand goes up. Although others become uncomfortable as she tearfully shares details of her pain, they wouldn't have it any other way. They think she needs their compassionate understanding as she works toward recovery.

Some of the people in the church wonder why an attractive, twenty-eight-year-old woman is unable to maintain relationships or hold down a job. Of course, no one raises those issues with her, for fear of adding to her burden. Instead, they help her financially when she can't pay her bills and provide a listening ear when she loses a boyfriend.

The pastor has suggested to Cindy that she undergo counseling to help her deal with the bitterness and pain she has shared with the congregation. But she says that the pain is too intense and that it would be too overwhelming for her to confront those issues just now. Consequently, prayer and expressions of love continue to be poured upon Cindy. After all, she was abused as a child.

Many of us, like Cindy, subtly manipulate others by repeatedly reminding them of our pain. By doing so, we avoid accountability for our actions, and we may even find ourselves reaping short-range benefits from the compassion of others. Long-range rehabilitation, however, is forestalled.

REPARATION OR RUIN?

When the benefits of remaining a victim are perceived to be greater than the benefits of taking personal responsibility, motivation to move forward is lost. This dynamic can be observed from both an individual and social standpoint. According to black writer Shelby Steele, African Americans in particular have been negatively impacted by social policies that encourage passive victimization rather than active responsibility.

In his book *The Content of Our Character,* Steele contends that the policy of affirmative action has done more to harm the advancement of black individuals than to help and has undermined the desperate need for individual responsibility. He encourages blacks to stop blaming racism for their problems and stop using it as a tool for manipulating power through guilt.

According to Steele, affirmative action, which was advanced as a means of righting past wrongs, has served to compound the cultural myth of black inferiority. It says that legislation is needed to accomplish what blacks are unable to do for themselves. What was intended for good, therefore, negatively affects those it was designed to help, because the policy implies that African Americans are unable to advance without special rights. These "rights" are then used as a weapon to force advancement, thus eliminating the need for personal discipline and responsible living. As Steele points out:

> This is the logic by which many blacks, and some whites, justify affirmative action—it is something "owed," a form of reparation. . . . But this logic overlooks a much harder and less digestible reality, that it is impossible to repay blacks living today for the historic suffering of the race . . . the concept of historic reparation grows out of man's need to impose a degree of justice on the world that does not exist. Suffering can be endured and overcome, it cannot be repaid. Blacks cannot be repaid for the injustice done to the race, but we can be corrupted by society's gestures of repayment.[1]

Many within the black community believe that such government policies have hindered their struggle to achieve equal standing in society because they encourage passive victimization rather than active responsibility. Their observations reinforce the need to emphasize personal responsibility as the key to advancement. Whether we are encountering racism, poverty, childhood abuse, physical disability, or any other current of resistance, we must learn to hold ourselves accountable to move forward.

No Victims Allowed

During the 1960s, William Glasser wrote a book titled *Reality Therapy* that challenged the conventional approach to psychological therapy and psychiatric treatment. Then, as now, the average professional counselor and therapist operated under the assumption that the patient was a victim of unrealistic standards rather than an individual who exercised wrong or inappropriate behavior. Glasser and others rejected that premise after extensive experience and overwhelming success using a method called Reality Therapy.

Glasser found that when he treated his patients as victims of external factors, their progress deteriorated. But when he began holding them accountable for their choices and actions, dramatic recovery became common. Extremely severe cases—patients who had been in steady decline for years in psychiatric hospitals— greatly improved when treated under Glasser's premise that everyone, regardless of his situation, is responsible. Many of his claims stood in stark contrast to the wisdom of the day:

> Plausible as it may seem, we must never delude ourselves into wrongly concluding that unhappiness led to the patient's behavior, that a delinquent child broke the law because he was miserable, and that therefore our job is to make him happy. He broke the law not because he was angry or bored, but because he was irresponsible. . . . Because the patient must gain responsibility right now, we always focus on the present. . . . In Reality Therapy, therefore, we rarely ask why. Our usual question is *What? What* are you doing—not *why* are you doing it? Why implies that the reasons for the patient's behavior make a difference in therapy, but they do not. The patient will himself search for reasons; but until he has become more responsible he will not be able to act differently, even when he knows why.[2]

Glasser described how Reality Therapy transformed the rehabilitation rate at a Ventura institution for criminal women, as well as the recovery rate at a hospital in West Los Angeles for psychotic patients. Acknowledging personal responsibility was a primary factor in both situations. In a context of loving support and honest confrontation, scores of people regained hope and were freed from the taskmaster of victimization.

> The philosophy which underlies all treatment at the Ventura School is that mental illness does not exist. . . . We accept no excuses for irresponsible acts. Students are held responsible for their behavior and

cannot escape responsibility on the plea of being emotionally upset, mistreated by mother, neglected by father, or discriminated against by society. . . . When they tell us how unfortunate they have been, we accept this uncritically; but from the beginning, in a warm and firm manner, we tell them that while they are here they are responsible for what they do, regardless of how miserable, inconsistent, or unloving the past may have been. . . .

The staff of Building 206 no longer believe that mental illness exists; the patients can, therefore, do better if they can be helped to help themselves *slowly but surely act more responsibly.* . . . The great insight into their "illness" that many patients obtained did not increase their responsibility. When they understood why they were mentally ill, it made even more sense to them to stay as they were.[3]

It is not my purpose to comment one way or the other on the existence of mental illness or the long-range impact of dysfunctional upbringing. However, one thing is certain. Dr. Glasser and his colleagues gave people hope by refusing to allow them to remain victims to circumstance or "sickness." By insisting that they accept responsibility for their own life choices, actions, and attitudes, Glasser granted the patients the freedom to rehabilitate.

I have seen and read the stories of thousands who only acknowledge life's difficulties in order to justify their own wrong choices. Life *is* difficult. But that doesn't mean our effort to move upstream is hopeless.

A painful childhood does not give us the right to become bitter. Although we cannot make others acknowledge and repent of wrongs they committed against us, we can choose to forgive them and repent of our own vengeful spirit.

If I am waiting for another to seek my forgiveness and reparation before I can overcome my bitterness, I may never be free from my prison of hatred. If my circumstances must change before I can move ahead, I may never reach my goals. But if I hold myself accountable for my own rehabilitation and growth, I can choose to move beyond victimization toward personal responsibility.

We tend to be like the monkey who reaches into a jar to grab a piece of fruit. Once he grasps the prize, his fist is too large to pull back though the narrow mouth of the jar. Until he is willing to release the fruit, his hand will remain trapped. The desire to keep the fruit is the very thing preventing him from having it.

As long as we hold on to our victimization, perceiving its benefits to be greater than the benefits of personal responsibility, we will never be able to resist the currents of life. Whether encountering emotional distress, destructive habits, or relational strain, viewing ourselves as helpless victims prevents recovery. Not until we take responsibility for our own choices and their consequences can we gain hope of advancement.

BOTTOM LINE

Each of us makes lifestyle choices through the decisions we make. When we make wise decisions, we reap positive results. When we choose the way of the fool, we reap folly. The law of sowing and reaping is as real as the law of gravity.

Those who believe they have something to gain by remaining victims of past experience, present circumstance, or other people will refuse to accept personal responsibility for their own advancement. As a result, sought after recovery is prolonged, if not averted altogether. It is not until we take personal responsibility for our choices and their consequences that we can gain hope of advancement.

8
The Benefits of Purpose

Great minds have purposes, others have wishes.
Washington Irving

Take a few moments to consider your response to the following questions.

1. What is your overriding objective in life?
2. What obstacles must be overcome in order to fulfill this objective?
3. What notable achievements can you identify that have advanced this life objective?
4. Within this context, what specific things do you intend to accomplish within the next five years?
5. What steps have you taken to ensure the realization of these goals?

If you are like most people, you probably found yourself struggling to answer some or all of those questions. Very few of us have clearly identified what we hope to accomplish in life, let alone planned the steps necessary to get there. Yet, without specific goals and objectives, living a responsible lifestyle can be nothing more than meaningless duty and toil. With them, on the other hand, it can be exciting in the short run and rewarding over the long haul.

In his little book *A Strategy for Daily Living,* psychiatrist Ari Kiev summarizes his experience with helping people set goals:

> In my office practice and in my consultant work . . . I have repeatedly found that helping people to develop personal goals has proved to be the most effective way to help them to cope with problems and maxi-

mize their satisfactions. Observing the lives of people who have mastered adversity, I have repeatedly noted that they have established goals and, irrespective of obstacles, sought with all their effort to achieve them. From the moment they fixed an objective in their mind and decided to concentrate all their energies on a specific goal, they began to surmount the most difficult odds. Those who lead successful lives have made a disciplined effort to systematically pursue an objective rather than to drift about aimlessly with no objective.[1]

If you were to attend any corporate management seminar today, you would walk away with a notebook full of reasons to define your goals and methods for reaching them. In the business world, clear objectives and a plan for accomplishing them are a must.

On the first day of semester in a typical college classroom, the professor distributes a course outline and syllabus. The students know precisely what is expected of them, as well as what they will be learning during the coming weeks. This enables them to schedule time for the assignments and cram sessions for the tests. Without the clearly defined objective provided in the syllabus, most students would find the academic process frustrating and ineffective.

What is true in a corporate or academic setting is also true for individuals. Clear objectives and goals are essential if we hope to be effective in our private lives. When we aim for nothing, we usually end up nowhere.

Have you ever looked into your wallet at the end of a week and wondered where all the money went? How could those minor expenses have eaten up your wad so quickly? In much the same way, we may look back over the years of our lives and wonder what we did with all that time. Many come to the end of their life and find that they've spent it on unimportant things and have nothing to show for their investment.

PONDERING A PARABLE

It seems awkward to discuss personal ambition and goals in the context of biblical Christianity. After all, if we have a heavenly perspective we shouldn't dwell on earthly matters, should we? We generally emphasize the benefits of our future hope to the exclusion of our present responsibilities. But the Bible never suggests that we should passively wait for the next life. Rather, it urges a lifestyle of confident purpose in the here and now.

As we learned from our examination of Old Testament wisdom living, God intends for His people to use the abilities they have been given to bring Him honor. That principle can also be seen in the New Testament. On one occasion, Jesus shared a story that could easily have been taken from a business administration textbook:

> Again, it will be like a man going on a journey, who called his servants and entrusted his property to them. To one he gave five talents of money, to another two talents, and to another one talent, each according to his ability. Then he went on his journey. (Matthew 25:14-15)

I should point out here that we are talking about big dollars. Each talent was probably the modern-day equivalent of about $350,000. The boss was handing over heavy responsibility to his junior executives.

> The man who had received the five talents went at once and put his money to work and gained five more. So also, the one with the two talents gained two more. But the man who had received the one talent went off, dug a hole in the ground and hid his master's money.
>
> After a long time the master of those servants returned and settled accounts with them. The man who had received the five talents brought the other five. "Master," he said, "you entrusted me with five talents. See, I have gained five more."
>
> His master replied, "Well done, good and faithful servant! You have been faithful with a few things; I will put you in charge of many things. Come and share your master's happiness!"
>
> The man with the two talents also came. "Master," he said, "you entrusted me with two talents; see, I have gained two more."
>
> His master replied, "Well done, good and faithful servant! You have been faithful with a few things; I will put you in charge of many things. Come and share your master's happiness!" (Matthew 25:16-23)

So far, so good. Even Merrill Lynch would have been proud of this lot. Let's see how the third servant fared with his investment strategy.

> Then the man who had received the one talent came. "Master," he said, "I knew that you are a hard man, harvesting where you have not sown and gathering where you have not scattered seed. So I was afraid and went out and hid your talent in the ground. See, here is what belongs to you." (Matthew 25:24-25)

Notice that from the start this servant tries to pin the blame for his irresponsibility elsewhere. In fact, he points his finger directly at the master. In essence he says, "If you weren't such a demanding boss I might have been able to do something with this money. But out of fear, I decided not to take any risks." With a boss such as he describes, you have to feel sorry for him. Does the master go easy on the poor guy?

> His master replied, "You wicked, lazy servant! So you knew that I harvest where I have not sown and gather where I have not scattered seed? Well then, you should have put my money on deposit with the bankers, so that when I returned I would have received it back with interest. Take the talent from him and give it to the one who has the ten talents. For everyone who has will be given more, and he will have an abundance. Whoever does not have, even what he has will be taken from him. (Matthew 25:26-29)

He wasn't swayed by the servant's explanation. In fact, the master turns the lazy man's words back on him. "Since you knew what I was like, you should have known better. You're fired!"

The master expected something from each of his servants. The third servant was rebuked and punished for failing to fulfill that expectation. His failure to earn five additional talents was not what upset his master. Otherwise, the second servant would have been equally at fault. Rather, it was because he didn't make the best use of the one he was given.

In the beginning of the parable we are told that the master delegated to each servant according to his ability. He gave them only what he knew they could handle. The amount was secondary, but the handling was crucial. If the first and second servants were able to double their money, then servant three could have done likewise. The master would have even cut him slack had he put the money in a 5 percent passbook savings account.

Jesus used a common occurrence, delegation in a business context, to teach a spiritual lesson. It is that broader lesson which concerns us here. From that simple parable, we can glean important insights into biblical responsibility.

First, we do not all have the same capacity for accomplishment. Many people feel inadequate because they are not as bright or gifted as others, and they do not accept their own limitations. But accepting ourselves as God made us is crucial if we are going to set realistic goals.

Second, whatever abilities and gifts we do have were entrusted to us by God for His purposes. We have no claim to fame on our own. Remember, God gave us our natural abilities, and He did so for a reason. Acknowledge your abilities as God-given for service, not a basis for pride.

Finally, we are expected to use our abilities and gifts to their fullest. Rather than hiding our abilities in the ground out of a fear of failure, we must stretch ourselves to the limit and maximize what God has given us.

When we neglect to use our abilities to their fullest, God is not glorified. There is nothing spiritual about idleness. Although we may try to convince ourselves that it is based on humility, inactivity is nothing more than plain, old-fashioned laziness!

LIFE INVESTMENT STRATEGY

If we hope to invest our lives in things of lasting value, we cannot passively wait for the Lord to drop bricks on our heads. We must develop a plan of action that enables us to consistently move forward by utilizing the capacity for accomplishment granted to us by God. Using our "creation endowment" to the fullest brings honor to our Creator, so long as it is done in a context of obedience and humility.

There are three important aspects of a life investment strategy that, when consistently applied, reap tremendous long-range benefits. First, we must start at the end, basing today's goals upon what will be meaningful to us when this life is over. Second, we need to develop a flexible focus and be willing to adapt our objectives to life's unexpected changes. Finally, we must commit ourselves to deferred satisfaction, rather than immediate gratification.

STRATEGY ONE: STARTING AT THE END

I am one of those people who cannot allow a Christmas season to go by without watching some version of the Dickens masterpiece *A Christmas Carol.* I love seeing grumpy, stingy Mr. Scrooge transformed overnight into cheerful, generous Uncle Ebenezer. Even though I've seen the film many times, I can't help but smile whenever the cowering Bob Cratchet is given a raise for showing up late after "making a bit merry" the day before.

Perhaps the most profound message in this wonderful tale can be found in the reason Mr. Scrooge decides to change his ways. After investing in monetary gain and self-centered pursuits, he is given the opportunity to see how his life could end. Kneeling before a neglected grave bearing his name, he is struck by the realization that there are far more important things in life than the petty matters with which he has been consumed. From that moment Ebenezer begins putting his energies into a new set of priorities, not least of which is the celebration of Christmas.

The best way to place today's activities in proper perspective is to consider seriously where our present course is leading us. We must start at the end, like Scrooge, by honestly evaluating our daily lives in the context of eternal values. Are we investing our time, money, and energies in things that really matter?

It is easy to ignore the deeper questions of life in the midst of the hectic pace of the daily grind. But until we define our existence in a larger context, we cannot identify the target at which we should be aiming. Many would suggest that the specific target is unimportant, so long as you are aiming for something. However, our choices and actions are directly related to our overall goal.

For example, if your aim is to be happy, you will most likely invest your life in self-gratifying activities. If you believe meaning is found through higher consciousness and discovery of your inner self, you will probably invest your life in self-centered activities. If you believe there is no purpose in this life at all, you may easily be pulled into a cycle of self-destructive activities.

In order to view today's activities properly, we must define our overriding life objective. Once we have done that, we can set priorities and goals with that specific target in mind. There are several steps to clarifying our overriding life objective and our specific goals.

First, we must set aside uninterrupted time in a setting conducive to serious, prayerful contemplation. Focusing our lives involves more than jotting down a few Christian clichés about the meaning of life. Nor is it something we can successfully accomplish during a Sunday morning altar call at church. We must get away from our daily activities and the places we normally traffic in order to gain a clear perspective.

Second, we must honestly ask ourselves some tough questions. Though the list of questions may vary according to individual personality and opportunity, the general themes should be the same for all.

1. What gifts and abilities have I been given by God to use for His glory? (Can I teach, write, make money, reason, invent, influence people, build, draw, and so on?)
2. Based upon my current situation, what opportunities for using these abilities are likely? (Will I have children to rear, a career to advance, a church to serve, an education to pursue, and so on?)
3. What specific goals can I identify in the context of my abilities and potential opportunities? (Can I earn a college degree, start my own business, write a book, run for government office, and so on?)
4. What current obstacles must be overcome before I can realize these goals? (Do I need to attend classes, change jobs, heal a relationship, get out of debt, and so on?)

Third, we must attach a time frame to each of our goals. One of the primary reasons we do not reach our goals is that we put them in the "some day" category. We know we want to get there but don't hold ourselves to a timetable. In order to prevent our objectives from falling into the black hole of the indefinite, we need to set realistic deadlines for accomplishing them.

Finally, write them down. It is important to record our objectives and refer back to them periodically in order to reinforce our aim.

Starting at the end enables us to clarify our focus. Rather than be carried wherever the winds of life may blow, we can carefully keep ourselves on a predefined course.

STRATEGY TWO: FLEXIBLE FOCUS

Connie was on a fast track in her career. She was certain to reach top management without interruption. That is, until she and her husband discovered that they were expecting a baby. Suddenly, she was forced to reevaluate her goals.

Cathy, on the other hand, wanted nothing more in life than to be a mother, and her every goal revolved around the hope that she and her husband would have lots of kids. After years of trying and countless tests, she finally had to reckon with her infertility. Without her approval, the realities of life have prevented her from fulfilling a dream.

Both Connie and Cathy faced the realization that life is not always as we plan it. Unexpected events and circumstances can delay and even eliminate our ability to reach certain goals. How we respond to such instances makes all the difference in the world.

Though living responsibly involves setting and pursuing goals, it also means letting God be God. We cannot set our own objectives in concrete. Life is uncertain, and we do not know what the future holds. Should He decide to, the Lord could radically alter our course in order to fulfill His larger purposes.

Having a flexible focus means holding our dreams and plans with an open hand. If we allow the unexpected interruptions in our plans to make us angry or depressed, it is because we do not have a flexible focus. Should the realities of life force us to head in another direction, we are able to adjust our goals and move on. Rather than bemoaning the fact that our course has been altered, we can set new sights with excitement and diligence. Remember, our overriding objective is to glorify God in whatever we do. The specifics may change, but the big picture remains constant.

STRATEGY THREE: DEFERRED SATISFACTION

My wife and I recently spent the day at one of the many amusement parks located in southern California. I have loved roller coasters and six-dollar hot dogs since I was a little boy. But on that day with my wife I took my first serious look at what actually takes place during a day at the park.

First, we wait in line for several minutes before reaching the lady at the window. I pay her the money, draining my wallet in the process—and that's just to park the car. We then stand in another line to buy tickets.

After recovering from shock over the price, we walk all the way to the other end of the park, hoping to be among the first to ride "the world's largest roller coaster." Naturally, we are not among the first. It typically takes one to two hours of winding through the maze-shaped line, passing by the same love-crazed couple sixty-three times before getting the chance to ride.

The last time we attended the amusement park, we spent about six hours standing in line, and we were only at the park for a total of eight hours! By the end of the day, we had blistered feet, sun-burned skin, and an empty wallet. I had to ask myself, *Why?* Why would we voluntarily put ourselves through hours of "torture" in exchange for a few moments of fun? The answer is simple. We considered the thrill of the rides worth the sacrifice.

A dynamic was at work in our experience at the amusement park that carries over into all other areas of life. It is called "deferred satisfaction." By enduring the difficult, the pleasant is obtained. Without the former, we cannot achieve the latter.

Why does waiting in line at the local theater seem less frustrating than waiting in line to pay for your groceries? Why can you get a child to eat something he hates, such as broccoli, by promising him something he loves, such as a cookie? In both cases, the anticipation of something good makes the negative seem worthwhile.

I enjoy learning, but I don't enjoy academics. For me, school has always been a necessary evil. Yet after the thirteen years required to finish high school, I voluntarily went through seven more years of school to obtain college and postgraduate degrees. Why? Because enduring that which I do not like, academics, was a way to obtain what I enjoy, education. Few moments in my life have been as satisfying as when the president of the university handed me that hard-earned sheepskin.

It is our willingness to defer satisfaction that enables us to reach our goals. The extent to which we understand and accept this principle is directly related to the probability of our success. When we consider long-range benefits more important than short-range comfort, we will do what is necessary to get where we want to go.

The process of maturing includes the realization that immediate gratification is generally not possible and usually not profitable. Most things worth having cost something. Unless we are willing to pay that cost, there is no true satisfaction in obtaining them. When things get tough, we have two choices. We can go for immediate gratification, or we can endure the difficult and continue moving forward.

If we hope to reach our upstream ambitions, it is going to cost us. Healthy relationships cost commitment and selflessness. Financial security costs discipline and sacrifice. Emotional well-being may cost confrontation with painful memories. In each case, however, the long-range payoff is well worth the investment.

PURPOSE

Every four years, athletes from every part of the world come together to compete against one another in the Olympic Games. Some of these athletes leave the games with a gold medal, which signifies that they are the world's finest at their sport. Others go home without a prize, despite the fact that they gave their best effort. Both groups gain the realization of a dream: the honor of representing their homeland.

Each of those who enters the Olympic Games has to make tremendous personal sacrifice. Years of difficult training, careful eating habits, bruises, blisters, and even heartache all come before the glory. What is it that gives Olympic athletes the desire, courage, and stamina to endure years of pain and discipline in exchange for a few short moments of competition?

Each athlete, regardless of his sport, shares a common goal; to represent his homeland before a watching world. It is that objective that drives them to pursue personal excellence and become the best that they can become. Win or lose, the honor of wearing the national uniform makes years of discipline and sacrifice worthwhile.

As citizens of His kingdom, we have the opportunity to be God's representatives in the game of life. With a common purpose behind our various endeavors, we are compelled to give 100 percent to every task before us.

> Do you not know that in a race all the runners run, but only one gets the prize? Run in such a way as to get the prize. (1 Corinthians 9:24)
> Therefore, since we are surrounded by such a great cloud of witnesses, let us throw off everything that hinders and the sin that so easily entangles, and let us run with perseverance the race marked out for us. (Hebrews 12:1)

Something about having a meaningful purpose makes life worth living. Even when we experience the tough times, the knowledge of our larger objective keeps the fire alive. Like the Olympic athletes who push themselves to excellence in order to properly represent their flag, we can take heart in our every endeavor, knowing that we are doing far more than striving for personal gain. We are serving as representatives of the kingdom of God!

BOTTOM LINE

Few of us have clearly identified what we hope to accomplish in life, let alone planned the steps necessary to get there. Yet, without specific goals and objectives, living a responsible lifestyle can be nothing more than duty and toil. With them, on the other hand, it can be exciting in the short run and incredibly rewarding over the long haul!

There are three important aspects of a life investment strategy, which, when consistently applied, reap significant long-range benefits. First, we must start at the end, basing today's goals upon what will be meaningful to us when this life is over. Second, we need to develop a flexible focus and be willing to adapt our objectives to the unexpected changes life brings. Finally we must commit ourselves to deferred satisfaction rather than immediate gratification.

When we make bringing glory to God our central purpose in life, every activity takes on new and significant meaning. As representatives of His kingdom, we must use the gifts and abilities we've been given to their fullest.

9
Start Rowing

What we hope ever to do with ease,
we must learn first to do with diligence.
Samuel Johnson

I suspect that while reading these principles of responsible living you have found yourself torn between two opposing reactions. On the one hand you may have found yourself nodding in agreement and even identifying with the illustrations. Your secondary reaction, however, may have been less receptive. Life does not come in neatly wrapped difficulties that can be quickly solved. Whereas the principles themselves seem to be nothing more than common sense, they also seem too easy.

Sometimes the best way to clarify what you are trying to say is to explain what you are *not* saying. I am in no way minimizing the legitimate difficulties of life. As I have repeatedly emphasized, life is not easy. Those who glibly ignore the resistance created by life's trials allow themselves to be carried downstream by default. We must recognize and honestly confront life's pain if we hope to move forward. I cannot overstate this principle. However, neither can I stop there. We must hold ourselves accountable to move beyond recognition toward recovery.

It is precisely because life does not neatly package our trials that I have presented these principles as lifestyle habits rather than as quick-fix solutions. When the principles are consistently applied, they serve as a steady source of resistance to life's natural downstream drift. The earlier they become a part of our lives, the more likely we are to advance toward successful living. As we move further upstream, the water becomes more calm and the resistance less strenuous.

Although living responsibly may not be easy, it is simple. Unfortunately, we often undermine the simple path because it includes steps that are not easy. The gospel, for example, is a simple message. Many reject it, however, because it requires taking some difficult steps, such as an attitude of humility and an honest admission of need. In fact, we naturally find the simplicity of the gospel message offensive to our human pride. Yet, in God's economy, it is usually the simple that gives us the ability to confront the difficult.

PROVERBIAL PIGEON-HOLING

None of us likes to be placed in a box. When sweeping generalizations are made about our race, sex, religious affiliation, personality type, or any other aspect of our personhood, we react with indignation. After all, such pigeon-holing takes away our individuality. Despite our desire to maintain our uniqueness, however, using generalizations is sometimes helpful to understand human behavior. At least a very wise author named Solomon thought so.

The ancient book of Proverbs is replete with such generalizations. Solomon seemed to place people into two categories through his descriptions of the wise and the foolish, the wicked and the righteous, the lazy and the diligent, and so on. His pithy but practical illustrations about the two paths of life allowed little room for individuality.

> Lazy hands make a man poor, but diligent hands bring wealth. (Proverbs 10:4)
> A wise son heeds his father's instruction, but a mocker does not listen to rebuke. (Proverbs 13:1)
> A wise man fears the Lord and shuns evil, but a fool is hotheaded and reckless. (Proverbs 14:16)
> The tongue of the wise commends knowledge, but the mouth of the fool gushes folly. (Proverbs 15:2)

Solomon certainly understood that each of us has a unique personality, experiences, and needs. Yet, he chose to package his divinely inspired tips on human psychology in two distinct lifestyle categories. We can either view his generalizations as simplistically detached from reality or as clearly marked road signs to help us on the journey of life.

Just as Solomon used extremes to teach us the way of wisdom, we can better understand the way of responsibility by placing ourselves in one of two categories. Though it sounds simplistic, each of us tips the scales of his life, one choice at a time, in the direction of responsibility or irresponsibility. Thus, we must focus our attention on the patterns we establish through our day-to-day thoughts and actions.

FINDING THE PADDLE

I grew up in the beautiful state of Michigan. The famous Great Lakes surround the state, and thousands of smaller lakes can be found within its borders. In our county were dozens of places for fishing, swimming, and, of course, water skiing.

As anyone who has ever been pulled behind a boat can tell you, a strong engine is a must if you hope to get beyond drinking the lake. Few experiences are as enjoyable as racing along the water at high speed, feeling the bounce of the wake beneath you. And few experiences are as frustrating as running out of fuel in the middle of it all.

Running out of fuel is really no big deal, as long as you have a full reserve tank. On one occasion we did not, and so it was. At first, there was a sense of panic. The boat could drift into dangerous waters without the power of an engine to push it to safety. Dropping the anchor helped for a while, but you can only sit in the middle of a lake for so long. The only reasonable solution was to find the emergency paddle and start rowing back to shore.

It sounded easy enough. Unfortunately, since the only reason to keep a paddle in a ski boat is in case some idiot forgets to check the fuel gauge, it is rarely out in plain view. After thirty minutes, we finally found the paddle and began to row to shore. Finding the paddle enabled us to make it safely back to dry land. Unfortunately, many individuals never bother to locate the paddle when they get caught in the currents of life. They know that a paddle is only valuable if used, and using it is difficult. As a result, they passively drift into dangerous waters.

In this section, I have been attempting to identify the paddle of responsible living. Finding the paddle is the easy part. It requires accepting responsibility for our own beliefs, choices, and goals. Once that simple step is taken, the much more difficult process of application can begin.

USING THE PADDLE

In order to begin using the paddle principles to confront the currents of life, we must ask ourselves three reflective questions. First, what is the truth? Second, what are my choices? Third, what is my purpose?

WHAT IS THE TRUTH?

A recent Barna report revealed that 66 percent of Americans believe there is no such thing as absolute truth. Is it any wonder, therefore, that so few of us bother to address this rather unsettling question? It is difficult to be accountable for living consistently with the truth while hiding from its reality.

What hope can be given to Janice, who was rejected as a child due to her shyness, if the lie of her past cannot be confronted with the truth of her inestimable value in God's eyes? And what about Maria, who struggles with the truth of God's goodness in light of the cruelty of her father? If reality is limited to her individual experience, then there is no hope for recovering from the lie of her past. But if reality is expanded to include universal absolutes, both Janice and Maria have hope. We must confront the specific experience with the liberating truth of God's revelation.

Let's face it, there are things in each of our lives that we hide from the penetrating light of truth because it would hurt too much to reveal them. But we must force ourselves to seek the truth in all situations. We must ask ourselves some tough questions about our life maps. Are we attempting to avoid accountability by clinging to ignorance? Have we accepted truths that we find palatable, while rejecting those we consider unpleasant? If so, how do we expect to live consistently with reality?

As stated in chapter 6, we live according to what we believe to be true, whether or not that perspective is accurate. Discovery of and commitment to truth in all aspects of life is an essential first step toward a life of responsibility. Even when unpleasant, the truth is the only reliable guide for our journey upstream.

WHAT ARE MY CHOICES?

Our natural tendency as fallen human beings is to avoid responsibility for our choices, particularly when they bring troublesome consequences. Blame shifting began in the Garden of Eden, and we've had thousands of years to master the practice. Unfortunately, the "comfort" of victimization has replaced personal responsibility.

Our choices should be placed in two broad categories. The first includes all those that shift the responsibility for action elsewhere. We will label this box "victim choices." The second category involves choices that place the responsibility for action upon oneself. This box could be labeled "hope choices." In order to make hope choices rather than victim choices, certain unhealthy perspectives must be identified.

Victim choices grow out of a natural desire to avoid personal growth and accountability. They focus on individual rights rather than individual responsibility. People who make victim choices shift blame elsewhere and concern themselves more with what causes irresponsible behavior than what can be done to rectify it. They ignore active steps of growth and recovery by adopting passive attitudes of victimization.

Hope choices, on the other hand, grow out of an intentional effort to move forward on the river of life. Those in this category focus on what can be done *today,* rather than what should have been done *yesterday.* They emphasize personal responsibility and growth rather than personal satisfaction and comfort. They seek to find their part of the problem, so that they can be part of the solution. They replace victimization with hope by eliminating the need for easy solutions.

Holding yourself accountable for choices and their consequences is the second important step in a life of responsibility. When you begin making more hope choices than victim choices, successful living becomes possible.

WHAT IS MY PURPOSE?

Focusing our attention on long-range objectives gives us the motivation we need to endure short-term trials. It also provides us with a healthy perspective when we are tempted to digress into our naturally irresponsible ways. Therefore, we must continually address the question of purpose.

I have read many motivational books that encourage the reader to pursue a better life through intentional and disciplined enterprise. Yet the reader cannot maintain lasting inspiration because the primary objective is personal satisfaction and happiness. You see, those things are only realized when the focus of life transcends self.

Goals that center on personal gratification and selfish ambition have no place in the responsible life. We are accountable for how we invest our lives and for coordinating personal goals with our larger purpose of bringing glory to God. When our upstream ambitions are defined in a meaningful context, every activity has a focus.

Heading Upstream

As stated earlier, each of us desires to head upstream on the river of life. Whereas we all have different ideas of what it means to be upstream, there are some general themes common to all. They include:

1. The ability to develop and maintain healthy, constructive relationships with God, family, and friends
2. Growing spiritually, professionally, and intellectually on a consistent basis
3. Personal integrity and financial discipline, as well as the rewards associated with each

In short, it is those positive aspects of life that everyone hopes to realize but few seem to attain.

I have attempted to identify and explain the principles of responsibility which, when consistently applied, provide a means for moving toward those and other upstream ambitions. I can explain the principles and encourage their application, but only you, the reader, can translate them into your specific life situation.

In the final section of this book, you will read real-life examples of people who, for one reason or another, find themselves downstream. Life's currents have combined with irresponsible life patterns to push them further and further away from their upstream ambitions. I will draw upon these cases to highlight steps of responsibility that can be taken to counter their downstream drift. As with Solomon's proverbs, I hope these chapters serve as clearly marked road signs for your journey of application.

BOTTOM LINE

Finding the paddle of responsible living requires accepting responsibility for our own beliefs, choices, and goals. Once that simple step is taken, the much more difficult process of application can begin. When confronting the currents of life, we must ask ourselves three reflective questions of application. First, what is the truth? Second, what are my choices? Third, what is my purpose?

Section Four
HEADING UPSTREAM

*Once we have grasped the paddle principles,
we can begin a lifestyle of responsibility
and move upstream.*

10
Spiritual Responsibility

As the deer pants for streams of water,
so my soul pants for you, O God.
My soul thirsts for God, for the living God.
Psalm 42:1-2

We are spiritual beings. Unlike the animals, we were created with the ability and need to relate to God on a personal level. When that need is unmet, our lives are incomplete and a void exists in the pit of our souls. Like a starving man in search of food, we look for anything that will ease the hunger pangs. When we find it, we grasp it tightly and devour it. Unfortunately, not everything that temporarily eases hunger has lasting nutritional value. Hence, we set ourselves up for what could be called spiritual victimization.

Spiritual victims are those who allow themselves to become entangled in religious beliefs and behavior that are not based upon truth. Though the short-term hunger pangs may be satisfied, the long-term consequences are quite harmful. Stephen Arterburn and Jack Felton describe this dynamic in their book titled *Toxic Faith:*

> Toxic faith is a destructive and dangerous relationship with a religion that allows the religion, not the relationship with God, to control a person's life. People broken by various experiences, people from dysfunctional families, people with unrealistic expectations, and people out for their own gain or comfort seem especially prone to it. It is a defective faith with an incomplete or tainted view of God. It is abusive and manipulative and can become addictive. . . . Those with toxic faith use it to avoid reality and responsibility. . . .
>
> Toxic faith has nothing to do with God. It has everything to do with men and women who want to concoct a god or faith that serves

self rather than honors God. In short, toxic faith is an excuse. It is an excuse for an abusive husband to mistreat his wife because he believes God would want her to submit to him as if he was God. It is an excuse to put off dealing with the pain in life. It is an excuse to wait for God to do what He wants you to do. It provides a distraction through compulsive "churchaholism" or religious ritual.

Toxic faith is also a counterfeit for the spiritual growth that can occur through a genuine relationship with God. The toxic faithful find a replacement for God. How they look becomes more important than who God is. Acts of religion replace steps of growth. A facade is substituted for a heart longing to know God. The facade forms a barrier between the believer and God, leaving the believer to survive with a destructive addiction to religion.[1]

Spiritual victimization occurs when balance and truth are sacrificed in order to satisfy our personal quirks. Rather than apply principles of responsibility to our spiritual life, we passively allow ourselves to be carried downstream. As a result, we end up disillusioned with God, the only one truly able to fill our vacuum.

DOWNSTREAM

Some time ago there was wide coverage of a new group called "Fundamentalists Anonymous." Chapters were forming across the nation, claiming to give those who felt victimized by fundamentalist religion the opportunity to deal with their unique struggles and gain freedom from the restraints of an archaic and legalistic value system. I came across their newsletter, which outlined their goals, provided cases of those who have been helped, and gave strategies for overcoming the damage caused by fundamentalism. Throughout the newsletter, however, it was evident that the group was not simply trying to help people overcome an unbalanced religious culture. Rather, they hoped to "free" them from the entire Christian belief system.

I can identify with many of the concerns raised by such groups. My family was part of a narrow-minded religious environment while I was growing up. Guilt motivation, shallow messages, and emotionalistic appeals were commonplace in my early Christian experience. The God we were taught to fear cared more about our external standards than our internal peace. So, to a certain extent, I qualify as a "victim" of fundamentalism.

I'd venture to guess that most Christians would claim that they came from a less than perfect church background. We can all give testimonials of the impact of legalism or emotionalism on our lives. Unfortunately, many have abandoned the entire Christian worldview in reaction against denominational or individual excesses.

THOSE HYPOCRITES!

Alan became a Christian in a legalistic church that put more emphasis on the length of hair and the style of music than on the essential doctrines of the faith. Brotherly love was almost entirely overshadowed by judgmental division, and one's spiritual depth was determined by his church attendance. Consequently, Alan went through the motions but never experienced a true relationship with the Lord or with fellow Christians.

Desiring to be a spiritual leader in the home, Alan faithfully observed and enforced the mandates taught by his church. The kids were expected to maintain certain standards of Christian living and remain separate from the contaminating influence of the lost world. Unfortunately, a wall of separation also rose within the family. The older they got and the more their questions went unanswered, the less interested the kids were in Dad's religion.

After twenty years of blind faith, Alan himself began wrestling with the tough issues of life. The religion he thought provided all the answers now only seemed to pose perplexing questions. He became frustrated with his inability to bridge the gap between his mind and his beliefs and with his lack of "personal relationship" with the Lord. He also became angry with the hypocrisy and judgmental attitudes in the church, which seemed to have developed a wedge between Alan and his children. He eventually left his church and even went so far as to abandon Christianity altogether.

Unfortunately, Alan avoided dealing with the real source of his struggle by blaming "those hypocrites in the church." Even though his church was guilty of legalism, Alan himself had been legalistic and hypocritical. Despite the fact that his pastor did not encourage him to do so, Alan had every opportunity to examine the reasons for his faith. Developing a strong relationship with his children was Alan's job, but he neglected his responsibility. Rather than identifying and addressing his own wrong choices and priorities, however, Alan has chosen to blame the church. He has self-righteously washed his hands of the hypocrites. He has also rejected the one who still waits for a relationship with him.

BURNOUT

Roy is taking a spiritual leave of absence. The last thing he wants to do at this point in his life is to be involved in another church building project, visitation program, fund-raising banquet, bus route, choir musical, deacon board, Sunday school contest, or prayer breakfast. He has already paid his dues to organized religious service, and it is time for a break.

Shortly after becoming a Christian, Roy and his family became 120 percent involved in the local Bible-believing church. He was immediately recruited by the pastor to "get involved in the work of the Lord." If it is true that 80 percent of church work is done by 20 percent of the people, Roy was definitely in the latter group. Still young in the faith, Roy began to equate spiritual growth with Christian service. After all, the pastor emphasized *working for* the Lord and seldom mentioned *relating to* the Lord.

Eventually the emotional burden and physical exhaustion caught up with Roy. The never-ending job of building a church drove him to the point of burnout. Today, he has no idea what it means to rest in the Lord because *rest* is not a word Roy associates with his spiritual life.

GUILT

Anthony grew up attending a parochial school. He can still recite the various creeds and church regulations from memory. He knows more about Christian dogma than he cares to recall. In fact, it is the very dogma he was forced to learn that drove him away from the church. No longer able to handle the guilt and condemnation heaped upon him by the nuns and priests, he searched for a more accepting spiritual haven.

At first, Anthony avoided spiritual issues altogether. He associated God with guilt. The church was nothing more than a keeper of the list of rules and regulations that, when violated, would condemn him to hell for eternity. Rather than expose himself again to those feelings of fear, Anthony found it easier to avoid all religious involvement.

But the void in his soul would not allow Anthony to remain idle forever. He began searching for something less rigid that allowed him to be himself. He wanted to follow the promptings of his heart, rather than the mandates of some ancient book. Anthony found what he was seeking in the new age movement. He has rejected the existence of absolute truth, replacing it with a pantheistic worldview. Although he finds the rational contradictions of his new religion troubling, at least there is no guilt. He now has the best of both worlds—guilt-free existence and spiritual experience. His hunger pangs have lessened, and the only casualty is truth.

RELIGIOUS ASSOCIATION

Those of us who have experienced religious excesses in one form or another tend to assign certain characteristics to God by association. If we were part of a dogmatically legalistic group, we perceive God to be a cosmic killjoy. If we were involved in an emotional congregation, we may confuse our feelings with the voice of the Lord. If our minister regularly used guilt as a means to motivate us toward clean living, God may be someone to fear when we fail rather than one to whom we can go for forgiveness and restoration.

When our misperceptions about God color our understanding of the truth, our spiritual lives become more frustrating than fulfilling. Rather than attempt to identify the errors and draw a more accurate map, however, many abandon the pursuit altogether. Seeing themselves as spiritual victims, they retreat from the religious context and try to fill the void in another manner. For some, bitterness and anger force their way into the vacuum meant to be filled by relationship with God.

DISILLUSIONMENT

Disillusionment occurs when our hopes and expectations are dashed on the rocks of reality. Children experience disillusionment when they see inconsistencies in their parents or their ideals are crushed. Most eventually mature enough to realize that Mom and Dad are only human and that they did their best. Others allow their disappointment to fester until it becomes anger, holding childish grudges until the grave. They sacrifice relationships to their unwillingness to accept the reality that no parent is perfect.

I have observed this dynamic in the way people relate to God. They establish a set of expectations of Him that are inconsistent with who He has revealed Himself to be. Rather than enjoying a relationship with the God who is, they become bitter about who He is not.

The harsh realities of life are often the cause of disillusionment with God. We want Him to protect us from harm and give us a life of ease. Though we hope for a genie in a bottle to grant our every wish, when we open our eyes we can see that God is the sovereign Creator who can use difficulties in life to accomplish His purposes.

LIFE, NOT GOD, IS UNFAIR

I have some dear friends named Von and Joann Letherer. Throughout their thirty plus years of marriage, Von and Joann have sacrificed a great deal in order to fill "behind the scenes" roles in various Christian ministries. They are two of the most unselfish people I have ever known, and their love for God shines for all to see. What few see, however, is the intense suffering they encounter on a daily basis.

Von has hemophilia, a disease that prevents the natural healing processes from occurring in his body. He has been required to receive blood plasma from literally thousands of donors over the past several years, putting him in a high-risk group for contracting AIDS. Each time Von becomes ill, fear strikes the heart of Joann. Many hemophiliacs have already died of AIDS, and she is just waiting for the day one of his tests will turn up positive.

In addition to the emotional stress, many years of incomplete healing have left Von in constant physical pain. Just getting out of bed is a struggle, and making it through the day a triumph. The Letherers have also been victimized by ministry scandal, leading to financial setbacks and unfair accusations. Despite their difficulties, however, Von and Joann have remained committed to the Lord. In fact, they attribute their very survival to His grace.

Why is it that people such as the Letherers make their relationship with the Lord a priority despite serious suffering, whereas others abandon ship over the least frustration? Based upon the conversations I've had with Von and Joann, I believe it is because they have learned the difference between life's being unfair and God's being unfair.

In *Disappointment with God,* Philip Yancey describes his conversation with one man who, like the Letherers, suffered extreme difficulties in life. His wife was struck with cancer, and he developed complications from a head injury. Still, he refused to give up his relationship with God by becoming bitter at the injustice of life. When asked why, he responded with this explanation:

> The reason is this. I learned, first through my wife's illness and then especially through the accident, not to confuse God with life. I'm no stoic. I am as upset about what happened to me as anyone could be. I feel free to curse the unfairness of life and to vent all my grief and anger. But I believe God feels the same way about that accident— grieved and angry. I don't blame him for what happened.
>
> I have learned to see beyond the physical reality in this world to the spiritual reality. We tend to think, "Life should be fair because God is fair." But God is not life. And if I confuse God with the physical reality of life—by expecting constant good health, for example—then I set myself up for a crashing disappointment. . . .
>
> If we develop a relationship with God apart from our life circumstances, then we may be able to hang on when the physical reality breaks down. We can learn to trust God despite all the unfairness of life. Isn't that really the main point of Job?[2]

Life is unfair, but God isn't. The sooner we understand the difference, the less likely we will be to confuse the harshness of living with the God of life.

CREATOR OR FATHER?

If you were to enter the average church and ask the congregation the simple question, "How many of you believe in God?" virtually every hand would be raised. The same would probably occur if you posed the question to a group of unchurched individuals. If you were to follow up by asking them to describe the God they believed in, however, a few may begin to squirm. If you pushed them to summarize the quality of their relationship with this God, you may encounter blank stares.

A recent national survey revealed that nine out of ten Americans truly believe in God. However, when asked if they contemplated God or religion when confronting moral issues, most people answered that they do not.

Belief in God is only as practical as its impact upon our day-to-day experience. Nearly everyone acknowledges the existence of God. This could be compared with acknowledging the existence of our physical father. All of us recognize that we have or had a biological father. It would be lunacy to suggest otherwise. Even if we have never met him and know nothing about him, we have no doubt as to his existence. However, that belief does not mean we know or love our father.

There is a vast difference between believing in God the Creator and knowing God the Father. Truly knowing Him requires that we discover what He has revealed about Himself. We need to learn to know Him as He is rather than as our experiences have made Him out to be. In short, we must allow the truth in His Word to replace any faulty details on our spiritual maps.

Unfortunately, many who have been "victimized" by legalism, false teaching, guilt manipulation, or any other source of spiritual misinformation blame-shift their way out of correcting the problem. But blaming another person, institution, or situation for one's spiritual anemia does nothing to improve matters. Developing a healthy relationship with the Lord is the responsibility of each individual.

HEADING UPSTREAM

Each of us has a choice about his or her spiritual life. We can either allow ourselves to remain victims of the currents of misperception and disillusionment, or we can develop a balanced, healthy relationship with God, which is based upon truth. In order to do so, several steps may be necessary.

FIRST: IDENTIFY THE ERRORS

Suppose you were to challenge the premise of an atheist by asking Him to describe the God in whom he does not believe. Chances are pretty good that he will describe something other than the biblical picture of God. It would be appropriate to join him in his disbelief, since the god he describes does not exist.

The same is true in the case of certain views of God held by Christians. Religious association may have caused them to paint a picture that does not reflect God's true character. Consequently, it is necessary to reject the false notion of God in order to know Him as He truly is.

Spiritual maturity is a lifelong process of replacing lies with truth. But before errors can be replaced, they must be identified. The best place to start is to pinpoint the source of your frustration. If you feel guilty every time you think of God, it may be because you were raised in an environment that overemphasized judgment, so you need to learn the truth of God's grace. If you are unable to rest in the Lord, perhaps you confuse relating to God with working for Him.

It may be helpful to spend time with another Christian who seems to have a balanced, committed spiritual walk as you go through this process. (Avoid those with a long-faced piety who consider relationship with God to be a deep, mystical experience. Find someone who has his or her feet on the ground!) Ask him to help you discover the errors in your map. Tell him the areas in which you struggle. Who knows, he may have gone through a similar experience on his own journey.

SECOND: DISCOVER THE TRUTH

Once you have identified the errors, you must discover the biblical description of God's character and the path by which He can be approached. For those who question scriptural authority, the first step is to seriously investigate the claims and validity of the biblical text. Many hide behind intellectual camouflage in order to avoid personal confrontation with the Christian message. As G. K. Chesterton put it, "The Christian ideal has not been tried and found wanting. It has been found difficult; and left untried."

For those who have already embraced the Bible as God's revealed Word, it is necessary to redraw your map of spiritual understanding with its truth. It is not our purpose here to investigate all aspects of God's character. Volumes have been written to aid the Christian in his pursuit of the knowledge of God. Suffice it to say that the more you learn about Him, the more you will desire relationship with Him.

THIRD: CHOOSE RELATIONSHIP, NOT RITUAL

Once you have gained a better understanding of the Person God has revealed Himself to be, you are ready to build a relationship with Him. But don't substitute religious ritual for relationship. There is a distinct difference between the two.

The day my wife and I married, we expected to work at building a lasting relationship. Neither of us considered the marriage ceremony the key to domestic harmony. We knew that a successful marriage requires mutual commitment and honest communication. Although we could remain legally married without those things, we would not have a healthy relationship.

It is the same with your relationship to God. Though you may participate in religious ceremony, that does not mean you have a relationship. Commitment and communication are key elements to a healthy and meaningful relationship with the Lord. He is a personal God, not an impersonal force. And He desires to commune with us as a loving Father with His children.

SUCCESS

Scott grew up in a religious environment in which godly living was presented in terms of arrogant separation from the lost and liberal. He was taught to flee worldly vices such as movies, dancing, long hair, and contemporary Christian music. Although there was an emphasis upon salvation by grace apart from works, the list of dos and don'ts after salvation was enough to sour the sweet prospect of abundant life. It was at the point when his Christian life seemed most sour that Scott and I talked.

As a bright, sensitive young adult, Scott had grown weary of judging and being judged by others. He was tired of the guilt feelings associated with his religious experience. He wanted to embrace those of a different perspective, rather than avoid them. His non-Christian friends seemed to be good people, and he saw no reason to view them with suspicion or as prospective victims of a timid evangelization effort. The hypocrites he had been taught to respect as spiritual leaders, on the other hand, seemed in desperate need of renewal. As we spoke, it became evident that Scott was ready to throw the baby—Christianity—out with the bathwater—legalism and hypocrisy.

Because he knew that I had come from a similar background, Scott felt comfortable honestly telling me his frustrations. I could identify with his feelings of disillusionment. It is difficult to recognize and begin to counter the imbalance of a legalistic upbringing. More often than not, unfortunately, rather than seeking balance in their spiritual journey, people forsake the struggle altogether. Scott was no exception. He was ready to abandon Christianity as he reacted against the rigidity of those who professed its message.

I shared many of the principles discussed in this chapter with Scott during our conversation. He was about to become a passive victim to the current of religious excess by refusing to resist its pull. I challenged him to confront the dysfunction of his past rather than avoid it. Our conversation went something like this.

Kurt: "It sounds as if you are ready to reject Christianity altogether rather than find a balance."

Scott: "If what I've seen is what Christianity is all about, I want nothing to do with it. My non-Christian friends are more sincere and less judgmental than any of the church people I've known."

Kurt: "But it's irresponsible to reject Christianity based solely upon the inconsistency and failure of its adherents. *You* must sincerely investigate what the Bible teaches. You cannot assume that the imbalance you've observed represents its true message."

Scott: "But those hypocrites in the church read the Bible, and the preachers teaching it equate legalism and rigidity with godliness. Who needs a book full of finger-pointing and judgment? I certainly don't."

Kurt: "But blind rejection of the Scriptures is just as irresponsible as the blind acceptance of legalism you've discerned in others. If you look at the whole Bible and at the teachings of Jesus in particular, you may be surprised at just how far off some people are when it comes to representing biblical themes. Trust me, real Christianity has little to do with what you've seen. Don't jump ship until you know where it is heading."

I went on to recount my own story of departure from a similarly rigid religious subculture and how I came to realize that relationship with God is far too important to neglect due to a childish grudge. People will continue to misrepresent the Bible and its message. Yet each of us can choose to move beyond disillusionment toward a healthy relationship with the Creator.

Not long after our conversation, Scott began studying the Bible for himself. He stopped relying on what he had been taught by others and was surprised to discover the simplicity and depth of the biblical message. He found that many of the things he had been taught were conspicuously absent from his readings. Soon he began learning how to distinguish between the cultural taboos of his denomination and the substantive absolutes of the Word. Scott began rebuilding his relationship with God based on an accurate map, eliminating much of the frustration that came from trying to follow faulty directions.

The road to a healthy relationship with God has by no means been an easy one for Scott. He will continue to grope his way through many of the issues of his spiritual past. But he is a success story nonetheless. Confronted with the current of disillusionment and religious excess, he overcame the downward trend of his spiritual experience. Truth is replacing error, relationship is replacing ritual, and he has become a willing recipient of God's love and grace.

BOTTOM LINE

Each of us has a choice regarding our spiritual lives. We can either allow ourselves to remain victims of the currents of misperception and disillusionment, or we can develop a balanced and healthy relationship with God that is based on truth. Nothing else will satisfy the hunger within our souls.

11
Relational Responsibility

And let us consider how we may spur
one another on toward love and good deeds.
Hebrews 10:24

After creating Adam and placing him in a paradise called Eden, God made an interesting statement about the state of man. Despite perfect harmony with nature, daily communion with his Creator, and regular afternoon naps, something was missing in Adam's life. "The Lord God said, 'It is not good for the man to be alone. I will make a helper suitable for him'" (Genesis 2:18).

God never intended for us to go through life in solitude. He designed us to seek and maintain relationship with other members of the human family. Even fellowship with the Lord Himself is not enough to entirely satisfy our hunger for intimacy. We need one another! Whether we openly acknowledge it or not, each of us longs for acceptance, love, and companionship from other people.

Unfortunately, that longing can blind us to the reality of unhealthy, even harmful relationships. Our desire to be accepted and loved by others can motivate patterns of irresponsibility in how we relate to our family, friends, and associates. Lacking the tools necessary to build strong relationships, we accept frail substitutes.

DOWNSTREAM

There is no such thing as a perfect relationship. Conflict, minor irritations, and even full-blown arguments can all be part of a healthy friendship, marriage, or family union. However, there is a vast difference between a generally healthy relationship that includes some unpleasant dynamics and a genuinely unhealthy relationship that is destructive to everyone involved.

The popular labels are "dysfunctional" and "co-dependent." The root problem is a failure to apply principles of responsibility in relating to others. The result is a society full of downstream relationships.

WHY WON'T HE CHANGE?

Karen is married to Mark, "a wonderful man" who has some rough edges. As a child of an alcoholic, Mark was never taught how to treat others with respect or keep a commitment. His only example of fatherhood was an abusive, manipulative man who cheated on his wife. As one who has always been drawn toward hurting, needy individuals, Karen entered into a union with Mark, hoping to help him overcome his painful past.

Mark quickly developed many of the same relational patterns his father had displayed. When it came to personal sacrifice, he expected much of Karen but little of himself. Never satisfied with the efforts she put forth to please him, Mark made a point of embarrassing his wife with sarcastic and demeaning comments whenever they attended church or other social gatherings. Karen longed to be cherished by her husband as other women at church were, rather than described as "the old ball and chain."

Despite Mark's attitude toward her, however, Karen remained committed to him. *After all,* she thought, *how can a man with such painful childhood memories be expected to meet my emotional needs?* He had many needs of his own, and Karen was determined to be the one who would counter his negative background by being a positive, loving wife. In the name of unconditional love, Karen willingly endured mistreatment and disrespect.

Karen began asking the Lord to work healing in Mark's life and to change his heart toward her. She did not know how much longer she could take the neglect at home or the public disdain. Little by little, her dreams of a happy family life were crumbling, and she was starving for Mark's acceptance. *I have given so much love,* she thought, *why won't he change?*

Mark did begin to change—for the worse! He began coming home late from work without explanation. Karen suspected that he was seeing another woman but refused to allow herself to believe it. Karen remembered hearing Mark express hatred toward his father for cheating on his mom, and she knew he would not do the same thing. Unwilling to confront him, however, Karen lived with constant uneasiness. She just continued asking God to change him.

Karen was invited by a friend to attend a seminar that addressed some of the problems she was experiencing with Mark. She learned that it was wrong for her to ask the Lord to change him. Instead, Karen needed to allow God to change her. She was told that she needed to ask Mark's forgiveness for her self-righteous attitudes and learn to accept him the way he was. Karen went home with a renewed commitment to unconditional acceptance of her husband.

On the advice she had been given, Karen confessed her judgmental attitudes to Mark and asked him to forgive her for expecting more from him than he was able to give. She reaffirmed her commitment to meet his needs and promised never to question his actions again. As a result, Karen experienced an immediate sense of release from the stress of needing to see him change, and Mark was pleased with his increased freedom. But the relationship remained unhealthy. Mark has never suffered any consequences for his actions, and Karen has remained a neglected, disrespected wife. Both remain "comfortably" irresponsible.

THE BEST SON IN THE WORLD

Jeremy loves his mother very much. Even though he is very busy with his job, he calls her every few days just to see how she is doing. They have always been close, and she brags to the other ladies at church about what a thoughtful son she has. He cares about her and is always available, whether she has a crisis or just needs to talk. Jeremy is the best son in the world!

There were a few occasions when the relationship between Jeremy and his mother was threatened. The first was when Jeremy wanted to marry a young lady named Jill. They were madly in love and had stable jobs, with every reason in the world to tie the knot. That is, until Jeremy's mom expressed her opinion on the matter. Afraid that her son would neglect her after he got married, she stated in no uncertain terms that she did not approve of the young lady. She pointed out that, from her perspective, Jill was not right for Jeremy. Unwilling to risk prolonged tension between himself and his mother, Jeremy decided to break off the relationship with Jill.

The second threat occurred when Jeremy's boss offered him a large raise and promotion into management. The only stipulation was that he be willing to move to another state. Instead of living two blocks from his mother, he would live two states from her. When Jeremy told his mother about the opportunity, she cried. Knowing it would break her heart to see him go, Jeremy decided to sacrifice his own advancement in order to remain near his mother. The emotional bond between them was too close to endure such a physical distance.

Jeremy is still single, doing the same job, and living two blocks from his mother. Sometimes he thinks about where he might be had he made different choices. But then he remembers how much his mother needs him and how much he loves her.

THE BEST MOM IN THE WORLD

Rose has a son who refuses to grow up. Craig could be described as a twenty-six-year-old teenager. He sees life as one big party, neglecting any sense of responsibility. He can't manage his money, so she finds herself regularly giving him "one last check" to cover his credit card bills. Unable to hold down a steady job, Craig has found it necessary to live with Rose "just until he gets back on his feet"—for the third time in the past seven months. She agrees. What else can she do? After all, she can't very well let her son be homeless.

Craig is not without goals. His life ambition is to become an actor, so he spends a great deal of time and money auditioning for any and every role at the community playhouse. He has even taken a few spur-of-the-moment trips to Hollywood. Rose funded those trips in order to encourage his dream. She knows he doesn't have much hope of actually becoming a big star, but she can't tell him that. He needs to know that his mother believes in him.

On one occasion, Craig got into trouble with the law. Discouraged over his lack of success, he looked to the bottle as a source of encouragement. But he ended up being arrested for disturbing the peace. When the police called Rose, she immediately drove down to the station to bail him out. What decent mother could let her son spend the night in a smelly jail cell full of drunken bums?

Time after time, Rose has come to Craig's rescue. Being the good mother she is, she pays his bills, funds his dreams, and bails him out of trouble. When she considers all that she does for him, Rose can't understand why Craig doesn't grow up.

"TWO TO TANGO"

In our family of seven children we had many opportunities for sibling quarrels. Sitting in the back of the station wagon on the way to church was the perfect setting for typical childish fights. "She keeps touching me!" and "Quit it!" were part of most Sunday morning conversations.

My dad was a very patient man, and he would allow the foolishness to continue for some time. But sooner or later, he would glare into the rearview mirror at me and say, "Kurt, you better knock off that whining, or I'll give you something to whine about!" From where Dad sat, the fact that I was being victimized by my big sister didn't matter. He just demanded that I stop the bickering.

Unwilling to allow an injustice to occur without setting the record straight, I would immediately clarify the problem to my father. "But Dad, she started it!" Instead of coming to my defense as I had hoped, however, Dad would just utter that profound but confusing statement "It takes two to tango!"

Years later, I think I finally understand what he was saying. Even when someone mistreats me, my response is the key to resolution. I am a victim only when I allow myself to be victimized. How I respond determines whether I am part of the problem or part of the solution.

In the examples cited above, each of those who could be considered a victim has actually contributed to his or her problem by responding in an irresponsible manner.

Karen refuses to hold Mark responsible for his role in their marital problems, unnecessarily placing herself in the role of victim.

Jeremy responds to his mother's manipulation with passive compliance and as a result misses out on important life experiences.

Rose allows her son to take advantage of her because she refuses to let him suffer the consequences of his irresponsible lifestyle.

Irresponsible responses to the choices of others do not demonstrate love. Rather, they demonstrate a serious misunderstanding of what love is all about. A truly healthy relationship is one in which individuals hold each other accountable for choices and actions, even when doing so is painful.

Conditional Acceptance

It seems that Christians are particularly vulnerable to victimization in relationships because we tend to overemphasize unconditional love. We've been taught to love without reservation, to give without expecting anything in return, and to help those who are in need without question. Placing even the smallest demands upon those we love seems inconsistent with the biblical mandate on selfless, unconditional love. Hence, many allow themselves to be taken advantage of and treated with disrespect.

Countless relationships have been crippled by the notion that real love means accepting irresponsible behavior. But a distinction must be made between love and acceptance. As one of my seminary professors said, "A true friend loves you as you are but too much to let you stay that way."

I love my son unconditionally. No matter what he does throughout his lifetime, I will love him. However, there will be times when I will be unable to accept his behavior. Because I love him, I will discipline wrong actions and attitudes. Yet, my *conditional acceptance* of his choices will not detract from my *unconditional love* of his person. As long as I consistently demonstrate both, Kyle will grow up understanding that Dad loves him too much to let him do whatever he wants.

Both of these principles can be seen in the way God deals with His own children. He demonstrates unconditional love by providing salvation for all: "But God demonstrates his own love for us in this: While we were still sinners, Christ died for us" (Romans 5:8). But He demonstrates conditional acceptance by disciplining sinful behavior: "The Lord disciplines those he loves, and he punishes everyone he accepts as a son" (Hebrews 12:6).

When the distinction between these two principles is confused, a relationship may become imbalanced. If a husband places conditions and demands upon his wife without demonstrating love and affection, he will drive her away. If a wife accepts her husband's immoral activity in the name of unconditional love, she will become his enabler. In every healthy relationship, there must be a balance between unconditional love and conditional acceptance.

But placing conditions upon a relationship seems so cold and unloving! Isn't it better to endure injustice than to demand my rights?

I am by no means advocating that we "demand our rights" when it comes to relationships. However, there are times when we must demand *what* is right. For example, I expect my wife to remain faithful because it is right for her to do so, not because I have the right to a faithful spouse. Similarly, parents expect their children to obey because it is right, not because they deserve the obedience.

The same principle applies to all relationships. Manipulation, disrespect, abuse, unfaithfulness, and other harmful patterns should not be tolerated in a healthy relationship. Although we can continue loving the person, we must not accept behavior that will harm him and others.

CONSEQUENCES

Although it is impossible to prevent those we love from making foolish or sinful choices, we can allow them to suffer the consequences of their behavior. When we protect others from the consequences of foolish living, we prevent their maturation and ensure continued folly. If they burn themselves, however, they may realize the danger of playing with matches. And we may prevent a forest fire.

Earlier in the book we looked at the impact of our choices on the direction of our lives. The law of sowing and reaping helps us learn responsible behavior. The cycle of choice and consequence must be allowed to take place in the lives of those we love if we hope to see them learn responsibility. When we interfere with this cycle, we prevent their growth and create an unhealthy relationship.

In chapter 1 I described a situation in which the leaves from a neighbor's unkempt yard repeatedly blew onto our neatly raked lawn. No matter how hard we tried to keep our lot looking good, his lack of diligence prevented our success. There was a solution to the problem, however. We simply needed to build a fence to keep his junk from drifting onto our lawn.

When the unpleasant consequences of others' actions begin blowing into our lives, the worst thing we can do is clean it up for them. By raking their messes we enable them to continue their irresponsible lifestyle without consequence, and they will not grow. When my neighbor's junk began piling up in his own front yard, he was forced to begin taking care of his own mess.

How does one build a fence of protection in a relationship? By allowing those you love to suffer the consequences of their own irresponsible actions. Do not passively accept abusive behavior and unfaithfulness from a spouse. Refuse to pay an adult child's bills when he is unwilling to work for a living. Confront manipulation by demanding honesty in a relationship. Whatever the specific instance in which a loved one is acting irresponsibly, refuse to intervene and do not protect him from the consequences of his own wrong behavior.

Sometimes we are able to step back and allow the natural outcome of foolish living to impact a loved one. In such instances, no direct action on our part is necessary. We simply let the law of sowing and reaping take effect. However, there are instances in which our position in the relationship mandates our direct participation in the process.

In his excellent book *Love Must Be Tough,* James Dobson explains this dynamic in the context of marital crisis:

Adults will occasionally challenge one another for the same reasons they challenged their parents as children. Unconsciously, perhaps, they are asking the question, "How much courage do you have, and do you love me enough to stop me from doing this foolish thing?" What they need in that moment is loving discipline that forces them to choose between good and bad alternatives. What they don't need . . . is permissiveness, understanding, excuses, removal of guilt and buckets of tender loving care. To dole out that kind of smother-love at such a time is to reinforce irresponsibility and generate disrespect. It deprives the marriage of mutual accountability![1]

It is important that the principle of conditional acceptance be understood in its proper context. Building a fence of protection should be done because you love the other person and want a healthy relationship, not because you want to control him or end the relationship. Therefore, if it becomes necessary to build a fence to keep the junk out, always include a door to let the person in. Including a door means defining specific conditions that will facilitate a healthy relationship. It means being willing to forgive when you've been wronged, once the other person has repented. It means letting him know that you love him even though you cannot tolerate his harmful behavior. Remember, the goal is to encourage responsibility, not to punish or seek revenge.

Heading Upstream

It would be impossible to discuss every aspect of strong relationships in a single chapter. However, we can identify several broad principles that can help prevent relational irresponsibility.

Principle 1: Do not allow your need for acceptance to compromise your goal of healthy relationships. Many people are so desperate to be loved and accepted that they become entangled in dysfunctional relationships just to satisfy their need. Afraid of rejection, they find themselves tolerating irresponsibility and even abuse. But the short-term satisfaction is not worth the long-term pain. Only mature, healthy relationships can bring fulfillment and growth.

Principle 2: Learn to balance unconditional love for people with conditional acceptance of behavior. Part of being responsible in your relationships is the ability to love others unconditionally while holding them accountable for their actions. When one is emphasized to the exclusion of the other, the relationship becomes unhealthy and victimization occurs.

Principle 3: Commit yourself to doing what's best for the other person. Nothing will destroy a relationship faster than selfishness. When looking out for number one becomes more important than caring for the other person, severe conflict is inevitable. But when two mature individuals commit themselves to doing what's best for each other rather than satisfying their own needs, lasting companionship is guaranteed.

Sometimes doing what's best for the other person means confronting wrong behavior or pointing out an area of weakness. It may not always be pleasant, but as one very wise man pointed out, "as iron sharpens iron, so one man sharpens another" (Proverbs 27:17).

SUCCESS

My wife and I first met Bill and Jenny when they came to visit the newly married couples group that we were leading. They were young, attractive, and successful in their respective careers. Married only a few months, they seemed well on their way toward a lifetime of marital bliss. As we soon discovered, however, their life together was anything but ideal.

Only a few weeks after our meeting, Bill and Jenny began sharing their relational struggles with us. Spiritual and physical intimacy were absent from their marriage, and each found it difficult to respect or cherish the other. Jenny was suffering from severe depression because she feared that her marriage to Bill had been a serious mistake. Bill was feeling betrayed. He wanted a wife who would support him and encourage him on his road toward a successful career. Instead, he ended up with one who was critical and continually depressed.

It was easy to recognize the signs of a couple downstream on the rapids of marital disintegration. Manipulation, thoughtlessness, and unrealistic expectations governed Bill and Jenny's relationship. Neither was putting forth the effort necessary to improve matters. Each felt victimized by the other. Jenny lacked the romantic feelings necessary to give Bill the admiration he needed.

And Bill was so put off by Jenny's coldness that he quit trying to meet her needs. Both my wife and I shared the concern that this marriage would soon end in divorce.

Bill and Jenny, like many others, were faced with a choice. They could allow further deterioration of the relationship, justifying their passivity by shifting blame onto each other. Or each could be accountable for his or her own contribution to the marriage. Fortunately, both chose to grab the paddle of relational responsibility and started rowing.

After spending time with other Christian couples and attending several seminars on marital conflict, Bill and Jenny came to the realization that they were not alone in their struggles. Contrary to their mistaken impression, other couples also have difficulties. They found that the key to a successful relationship is not enduring romantic feelings or a perfect partner but the determination to make things work even during the tough times. Bill and Jenny resolved to work at the relationship rather than continue to justify their irresponsible patterns in the name of incompatibility. Jenny stopped seeking a magic feeling before expressing admiration and support for Bill, and Bill began loving the woman he married, rather than wishing for a cheerleader.

Today, Bill and Jenny provide a loving, stable environment for two beautiful children. They encourage other bewildered couples to hang in there and make it work. Theirs is not a perfect relationship, and they continue to have conflict. But Bill and Jenny have managed to avoid the heartbreak of further marital disintegration, and their home is one which brings glory to God. They are a success story, not because they have no problems but because they have chosen to confront and overcome them.

Bottom Line

We cannot accept irresponsible behavior in the name of unconditional love. A truly healthy relationship is one in which individuals hold each other accountable for choices made and actions taken, even when doing so is painful.

12
Moral Responsibility

This then is the dwelling place of sin—
the human heart. Here dwells our enemy.
John Owen

Of all the currents that create resistance in our lives, our own sinful actions are the most frequent and the most destructive. They are most frequent because they need no cause other than our own disposition toward evil. They are most destructive because we can convince ourselves that the blame lies elsewhere, using self-deceit as a means to avoid responsibility. As a result, the perpetrator and the victim become one and the same.

DOWNSTREAM

It is not individual sinful acts that create a cycle of destruction in our lives. Rather, it is the refusal to acknowledge them as such. By placing the blame for wrong choices on circumstances, past trauma, the devil, or any number of scapegoats, we blind ourselves to the true reason we are downstream. Because we never see ourselves as part of the problem, we never become part of the solution. Consequently, true victimization occurs. We become victims, not to outside factors but to our own presumptions.

CHEATED IN LIFE

Amy is an attractive, twenty-seven-year-old woman with two preschool children. She and her husband, Peter, have been married for nearly seven years. He is a hard-working man who loves his wife and children very much. What more could a woman want?

Amy dated quite a few men prior to meeting Peter but never found herself strongly attracted to any of them. On her second date with Peter, however, he announced his intention of marrying her. Amy just laughed. Many men found themselves quickly attracted to her, but it never lasted. But it was different with Peter. He was quite persistent, confident that it was the Lord's will for them to tie the knot. Although Amy had no particularly strong feelings for Peter, his obvious love for her prompted her to accept his proposal.

Over the years, Amy found herself going through the motions, but not truly loving Peter. "I love you" responses became empty and forced. It wasn't long before she fell into temptation at work.

From the very first day Amy met her new boss, Henry, she found herself feeling things about him that she had never felt for another man before. He seemed strong and self-assured, yet compassionate and caring. For several years, Amy forced herself to suppress an affection for Henry that came naturally. During the same period, her strained devotion to Peter disappeared altogether.

Amy discovered that Henry was struggling in his own marriage, and they began to talk about their difficulties. What began as innocent attempts to console one another led to that first kiss in his office and, eventually, adultery. Although she has attempted to break off their relationship on several occasions, Amy cannot bring herself to let him go. Henry is the only motivation to keep her going from day to day. For the first time in her life, she is experiencing true love.

Divorce is out of the question. Henry is a respected leader in his church, and Amy can't bring herself to hurt Peter and the kids. Amy is married to a man she can't love and loves a man she can't marry. She feels cheated.

ATTACK OF THE ENEMY

Week after week, Brian walks down to the front of the church at the end of the service to pray for deliverance. He is in a battle with the enemy, and he hasn't yet received complete victory from the Lord.

Brian's battle is with "the demon of lust." Despite his frequent requests for God to defeat the enemy in his life, he has been unable to overcome the temptations around him. Brian works the night shift in a local convenience store that sells pornographic magazines. Even though he asks the Lord to "bind the demon of lust" every night before he goes to work, he still finds himself drawn to those pictures. When attractive women enter the store, he can't keep himself from undressing them with his eyes.

Brian knows that good Christian young men should be able to control the lust of the flesh. He prays and reads his Bible every day, and he never misses a church service. His love for the Lord has never been stronger. But neither has his addiction to the female form.

Convinced that the Lord is going to overcome Satan in this area of his life, Brian continues to wait for victory. The pastor has suggested that he quit his job and work in a less tempting environment. But Brian thinks that would only rob God of the opportunity to demonstrate His power over the enemy. So, "the enemy attacks" continue, and Brian remains a victim.

EXCUSED

Mr. and Mrs. Jacobs did a pretty good job rearing their four children. Three of them grew up to become balanced adults and loving parents themselves. Jeff, the youngest, did not.

Jeff is physically abusive to his wife and children. They make him so angry with their ingratitude and selfishness, he says, that it is sometimes necessary to teach them a lesson. Recently, *he* had the opportunity to learn a lesson. Someone reported his behavior, and he was arrested for child abuse. Unfortunately, he learned the wrong lesson.

As part of his parole requirements, Jeff was ordered to attend weekly sessions with a professional counselor. He was assigned to a local psychiatrist, who immediately began to scrutinize Jeff's childhood. He asked probing questions about what kind of discipline Jeff's parents used, how often they demonstrated affection, whether or not they gave him the freedom to express himself, if they allowed him to be his own person, and so on.

After several weeks of examination, Jeff's counselor concluded that the reason Jeff was abusive toward his family was because his own upbringing was dysfunctional. In short, Jeff was not at fault for beating his family—Jeff's parents were the problem. Had they done a better job of meeting his needs as a child, Jeff would be better able to cope with his anger today.

From the "professional opinion" of his counselor, Jeff learned that he is an innocent victim of inadequate parents. Rather than acknowledging his guilt for the wrong he had done, he was handed an opportunity to shift the blame to his parents. Since the diagnosis came from a reputable professional, it had to be correct. Jeff is relieved that he is off the hook. But his family is still being abused.

Amy, Brian, and Jeff have all managed to avoid taking responsibility for their actions by shifting the blame elsewhere. Amy is cheating on her husband yet perceives herself to be cheated. She blames an unfair lot in life for her wrong choices.

Brian shifts the responsibility for his lust onto the forces of evil, rather than recognizing the evil within his own heart. Passively waiting for God to give him victory, he has failed to "flee youthful lust."

Jeff blames parental inadequacy for his abusive behavior. His counselor has granted him permission to see himself as a victim, rather than repent for victimizing his family.

No matter how obvious it may be to others, those who are involved in sin rarely see themselves as the problem. Something or someone else is always the cause of their moral irresponsibility.

THE TRUTH ABOUT US

Despite our attempts to explain it away, the truth remains; human beings are born with a sin nature. We are naturally drawn to evil, and enticed by what is wrong. The Bible declares it, history demonstrates it, and individual experience confirms it. Yet, we don't like to accept it because it is an unpleasant truth. Those who refuse to include this truth in their life map will find themselves at a serious disadvantage. How can we overcome a handicap we refuse to acknowledge?

It is difficult enough to deal with our sin when we recognize it. The apostle Paul hit the nail on the head when he described the inconsistency of the human will and its inability to overcome the weakness of the flesh:

> We know that the law is spiritual; but I am unspiritual, sold as a slave to sin. I do not understand what I do. For what I want to do I do not do, but what I hate I do. And if I do what I do not want to do, I agree that the law is good. As it is, it is no longer I myself who do it, but it is sin living in me. I know that nothing good lives in me, that is, in my sinful nature. For I have the desire to do what is good, but I cannot carry it out. For what I do is not the good I want to do; no, the evil I do not want to do—this I keep on doing. (Romans 7:14-19)

Paul does not attribute his moral failure to his circumstances, nor does he blame Satan for his inability to do good. Rather, he points the finger back toward his own sinful nature. The truth is, we sin because we are sinful. Outside factors can influence our behavior, but they cannot *make* us sin. The only one who can make us sin is us!

> But each one is tempted when, by his own evil desire, he is dragged away and enticed. Then, after desire has conceived, it gives birth to sin; and sin, when it is full-grown, gives birth to death. (James 1:14-15)

GOOD NEWS?

Part of the reason we resist accepting responsibility for our sinful choices is our desire to avoid guilt and condemnation. We perceive guilt feelings as a greater evil than actual guilt. As a result, we fail to experience the benefits of conviction.

Imagine yourself sitting in the office of your pastor or counselor. He walks into the room, notes in hand, and takes the seat next to you. You have been sharing details of personal struggle with him for several sessions and have been eagerly waiting for his opinion and advice. He immediately gives you the classic line "I have good news, and I have bad news. Which do you want to hear first?" You want the bad news.

"Well," he begins, "the bad news is that your life is pretty messed up." OK, you already knew that. What's the good news? "The good news is that it's your fault!"

Good news? To be told that your problems are your own fault can hardly be considered good news! Or can it?

If my difficulties are entirely due to outside factors, then I am entirely dependent upon others to fix them. If they are unwilling or unable to do so, my condition is rather hopeless. If, on the other hand, I am the problem, I can also be part of the solution. Hence, it is good news to know that I am the source of my own dilemma!

If this principle is true, why does it feel so awkward? I mean, when a person in pain comes to you for counsel, isn't it best to put your arm around him and comfort him, rather than point an accusing finger?

The appropriate question to ask is whether the person is seeking to be counseled or consoled. If he simply wants a shoulder to cry on, that's one thing. But if he desires to overcome his difficulty, that is another. When we confuse the two, we can create a sense of despair in those we seek to comfort.

Suppose you were my close friend and I came to you with a problem. After explaining my struggle, I ask for your advice. You can see that my own wrong choices have been causing my adversity. But you can't bring yourself to point out my error for fear that I will consider you insensitive. Instead, you listen, hug me, and cry with me. Rather than offer advice that may seem cold and uncaring, you affirm me in my struggle.

When I walk away from our conversation, I will likely feel more desperate than before talking to you. Why? Because your approach indirectly confirmed that my situation is hopeless. By crying with me without offering steps of action for resolution, you have pushed me deeper into despair. It would have been better for me if you had risked short-term rejection by pointing out my error. Doing so would have given me hope because I would see the potential for correction. The sting associated with conviction would be far outweighed by the prospect of resolution.

The tendency to give consolation to the exclusion of counsel has prompted a destructive mind-set in our society. Rather than hold one another accountable to a moral standard, we comfort one another to the point of avoidance. As a result, we have removed the concept of sin from our thinking.

THE HOPE OF SIN

During an era in which blame-shift therapy was the norm, acclaimed psychiatrist Karl Menninger asked society an important question with his book *Whatever Became of Sin?* He contended that our corporate shift toward a "no-fault" theology had pushed us into irresponsibility. Whereas the general disregard of individual accountability may have decreased feelings of guilt, it did not remove the consequences. By returning to an understanding of sin as sin, he explained, hope for improvement would be possible.

> The consequences of my proposal would not be more depression, but less. If the concept of personal responsibility and answerability for ourselves and for others were to return to common acceptance, hope would return to the world with it!
>
> Self-destructiveness can be lessened, painful coping efforts assisted, anxiety attenuated, not by mere reassurance or comforting words or minimization or distraction, but by a deliberate renunciation of apathy and a courageous facing of the responsibility for evil.[1]

Dr. Menninger's conclusions echo a common biblical theme, repentance. *Repentance* is a word that should inspire hope, not resistance. Certainly, it is uncomfortable in the short-run to admit our own guilt. Our pride compels us to avoid confession of wrong no matter what the cost. By doing so, however, we can acquire the hope and release that come from living consistently with what is true, regardless of how unpleasant that truth may be.

THE MOTIVATION FOR MORALITY

Motivation is a key factor to any behavior. Why we do what we do can often determine whether or not we will continue doing it. There are many reasons one could adopt for living a morally responsible lifestyle. Few of them, however, provide lasting motivation.

Some see morality as a means of obtaining God's favor, hoping to earn their way into heaven. But the Bible states clearly that our works have nothing to do with eternal life (see Ephesians 1:8-9). Those who pursue morality in order to acquire salvation will eventually find the uncertainty disheartening. Will I make it? Have I done enough good things to counter the bad? Is it worth the hassle when I have no guarantee? Such questions can destroy the motivation necessary to maintain a moral lifestyle.

Others strive to live a clean life out of a sense of duty. Afraid of the discipline associated with wrongdoing, they live by the list, never experiencing any sense of freedom and joy. No matter how devoted we may be, being good just because God said to provides little lasting motivation.

Lasting motivation for moral responsibility does come from the realization that it is the best lifestyle possible. Although it seems selfish, there is nothing wrong with doing right in order to obtain God's best for your life. He has revealed the path to fulfilled and successful living and wants us to take advantage of that knowledge.

I remain faithful to my wife because there are tremendous joys associated with a loving, committed relationship between a husband and wife. I could have more short-term excitement by pursuing numerous illicit affairs, but I would sacrifice long-term happiness in the process. That is a foolish and pointless trade!

Contrary to popular opinion, God is most glorified when we live fulfilled, successful lives. As stated in previous chapters, however, this success is not defined as obtaining our every temporal and selfish desire. Rather, it is living consistently with God's plan for us as those created in His image.

Viewing moral living as an opportunity to obtain God's best rather than an obligation provides the motivation to continue. Although temptation still occurs, its appeal is diminished in light of the larger picture.

Heading Upstream

The calm waters of the human spirit can be dangerously deceitful. Just when everything seems peacefully under control, a rush of temptation can quickly sweep us downstream toward destruction. Without warning, an upstanding, moral individual can become overwhelmed by evil within.

It takes a conscious effort to resist the current of our sinful nature. We must commit ourselves to several principles of moral responsibility that can help us avoid the trappings of sin.

FIRST: RECOGNIZE YOUR TENDENCY TOWARD EVIL

When you perceive yourself as basically good, you set yourself up for trouble. You cannot deal with your sinful nature until you acknowledge it. Denial of this reality only guarantees that the current of your nature will pull you into sinful behavior.

Realizing that you will most likely succumb to temptation due to your weak nature should warn you to avoid it at all costs! Don't arrogantly try to manage it; run from it. The Bible tells us to resist Satan, but flee from "youthful lusts."

SECOND: ACCEPT RESPONSIBILITY FOR YOUR OWN CHOICES

Do not attempt to shift blame for your wrong choices and sinful actions. Certainly, outside factors influence your behavior, but they cannot *make* you sin. Though it is healthy to recognize those things which have contributed to your anger, unhappiness, compulsion, and so on, they cannot be used to excuse your sin.

THIRD: KEEP SIGHT OF THE BIG PICTURE

Moral responsibility means placing a priority on doing what is right, regardless of our personal desires. It means going against our nature, which compels us to do what we desire, regardless of what is right. It requires deliberate commitment to the principle of deferred satisfaction, looking for long-range reward, not short-range pleasure.

SUCCESS

Earlier in this chapter, I told the story of Amy, a woman involved in an adulterous affair. Although she is cheating on her husband, she feels cheated in life. Amy, like many others, has rationalized her sin by placing herself in the role of victim. After all, if her husband were all that he should be and all that she needed, she would not need to search for fulfillment elsewhere. Amy is caught in the rapids of immorality with little hope of being rescued.

I know another woman whose story begins very much like Amy's but which has a drastically different ending. This young lady, whom we'll call Sally, also left her husband for another man. When asked how she, a Christian woman, could justify such immoral conduct, her response reflected an all too common perspective among the morally irresponsible.

"I felt that because he failed to fulfill his part of the marital bargain, I had the right to seek fulfillment elsewhere. In short, I justified my wrong choices by pointing the finger at his inadequacies."

After a period of self-centered and self-deceived pursuits, Sally came to the realization that her actions were inexcusable and morally wrong. She was confronted with the sinfulness of her actions, unable to justify them any longer. Sally ended her affair and entered counseling with her husband with the intention of salvaging the marriage. And although the marriage is stronger than ever today, the restoration by no means happened overnight.

When Sally first returned to her husband, she was not motivated by a magically renewed love for him. In fact, Sally told her husband upon returning, "I'm not returning to you because I love you but because I want to be obedient to the Lord." Sally took the step of moral responsibility because it was *right*, not out of respect for her mate.

The first year together after the affair was an extremely difficult period for both Sally and her husband. She was trying to rebuild respect for him, while he was trying to forgive her for the pain she had put him through. Despite the ups and downs, however, they have made it. Their marriage is restored because Sally was willing to take those first difficult steps of moral responsibility. She even finds herself more in love with her husband than ever before.

Unlike Amy's, Sally's story has a happy ending. She recognized her error and pursued the upstream path of moral responsibility. But even when restoration and victory come, the painful consequences of immoral conduct remain. Sally and her husband may never fully recover from the sting of her actions. Despite her repentance and his forgiveness, the emotional scars remain.

Nevertheless, Sally's testimony illustrates an important reality. No matter how far down the river of moral irresponsibility one travels, it is never too late to turn the boat around and start rowing upstream.

BOTTOM LINE

It is not sinful acts that create a cycle of destruction in our lives. Rather, it is the refusal to acknowledge them as sinful. By placing the blame for our unwise choices upon circumstances, past trauma, the devil, or any number of scapegoats, we blind ourselves to their true source.

13
Professional Responsibility

Labor disgraces no man,
but occasionally men disgrace labor.
Ulysses S. Grant

In recent years, Latin America has experienced a dramatic growth in the number of evangelical Christians. Once almost exclusively Catholic, it is estimated that more than 10 percent of the population is now Protestant. Along with this shift in religious association, economic advancement has begun. Many are suggesting that there is a definite link between the two trends. One sociologist observed that Latin American evangelicals are characterized by "effervescence in the chapel on Sunday and, beginning Monday, disciplined endeavor during the workweek."

In other words, there is something called the Protestant work ethic that induces professional responsibility. That work ethic has historically characterized the American work force, contributing to our unprecedented economic growth. Unfortunately, times seem to have changed. After conducting a survey of today's workers, James Patterson and Peter Kim summarized their findings with this sad commentary:

> The so-called Protestant ethic is long gone from today's American workplace. Workers around America frankly admit that they spend more than 20 percent (7 hours a week) of their time totally goofing off. That amounts to a four-day work week across the nation. Almost half of us admit to chronic malingering, calling in sick when we are not sick, and doing it regularly. . . . Only one in four give work their best effort. . . . But then, why should we? After all, half of us genuinely believe that you get ahead not through hard work but through politics and cheating.[1]

I did some quick math and found that the average person dedicates well more than eighty thousand hours to his profession over the span of a forty-year career. That doesn't include any overtime or any special academic training or commuting time. In reality, we may be spending more than one hundred thousand hours in occupational duties during the course of a lifetime.

When you consider the massive amounts of time we spend on the job, it's a shame that so few of us stop to evaluate whether or not we are being responsible in our professional lives. In fact, most of us view our jobs as a necessary evil, an unpleasant means of putting food on the table. I believe that is one of the primary reasons so many in our society are mediocre employees. Such a negative view of work hardly provides the motivation to give 100 percent consistently.

DOWNSTREAM

We in North America are blessed to be part of an employment community that considers the needs of staff to be a primary concern. In fact, one of the most sought after areas of expertise in the corporate world today is in personnel management. We've come a long way since the early part of this century when union riots and violence about inhumane treatment of workers were commonplace.

Whereas conditions have been getting better for the average worker, that same average worker seems less content than ever. Job dissatisfaction, a concept few would have imagined seventy-five years ago, has become a major issue among all kinds of employees. As a result, many people put themselves in the category of "professional victims."

Professional victims are those who feel cheated on the job. For one reason or another, they believe they have reason to gripe about the boss, the pay, the working conditions, the benefits, or the company politics. These inequities, whether real or perceived, become a source of agitation and a justification for performing below potential.

NOT TRYING

Kevin was unemployed prior to accepting his current job. In desperate need of a paycheck, he was grateful for the chance to work again. Excited about the opportunity to start fresh after several unpleasant experiences with previous employers, he began with high ideals and a drive to give 100 percent to every assignment.

After a while, however, things began to change. Kevin found it difficult to meet the high expectations of his boss. His ambition began to wane, and he abandoned his hope of advancement. "After all," he reasoned, "why push myself if I know I'll never be considered for a better job?"

The same job that at first gave Kevin reason to give his best effort is now a source of frustration. His hidden resentments are beginning to show in his attitude toward the boss and his lack of cooperation with his peers. Today the paycheck that Kevin was once so grateful to receive is taken for granted. It is also in jeopardy.

UNCHALLENGED

Sara has discovered that it is difficult to motivate oneself to do a job that provides little or no challenge. Filling out the same forms for the same reasons day after day is hardly what she envisioned herself doing after graduation from college. She dreamed of changing the world with her grand ideas. Instead, she finds herself changing typewriter ribbons.

Because she is bored, Sara has trouble giving her best effort to her work. Easily distracted, she often neglects to complete her assignments in a timely manner. But then, what can you expect from someone who is overqualified for her work? If the boss would just give her more interesting assignments, she would be more satisfied. Then she would be able to concentrate. Unfortunately, the boss hoards all the interesting work.

Sara is certain that if her job provided her with the challenges and professional satisfaction she needs, she would have the motivation necessary to be a top-rate employee. Since it doesn't and since her boss seems content to leave her unchallenged, she sees no good reason to improve her performance. After all, it is not her fault that the boss fails to recognize her potential.

DISCONTENTED

Few of us ever learn to enjoy our jobs. We allow a spirit of negativism to keep us from finding meaning in the hours we spend at the office or in the shop. It is as if we sign an agreement prior to accepting any position.

> I pledge to spend my time at work loathing every moment and to spend my time at home in anticipation of the unhappiness I will experience on the job. I promise never to be content in what I'm presently doing, nor to appreciate any new assignments. Under no circumstances will I ever be grateful for my paycheck, realizing that, regardless of my salary level, I am being paid less than I am worth. Finally, if I ever find myself enjoying any aspect of my job, I will resign immediately, and sue workmen's compensation for stress related difficulties.

Most of us can identify with that attitude. But such feelings of dissatisfaction and ingratitude are not only unnecessary; they are disobedient.

GOOD TIMES, BAD TIMES

During the decade of the eighties, jobs were plentiful and pay was good throughout much of the U.S. The marketplace changed from one in which workers had difficulty finding jobs to one in which employers were competing to hire a limited work force. Times were good in America, and more people had well-paying jobs than ever before in our history.

However, by the end of the decade, complacency became the norm in factories and offices across the country. As is all too common when things are good, attitudes became bad. An undercurrent of ingratitude and irresponsibility began to show itself through declining employee productivity and increased employee litigation. Workers did less and demanded more. Sadly, the real losers were the workers themselves.

Over the past fifty years, unemployment figures have gone up and down in cycles. So have employee attitudes. When times are bad, workers take any job they can find and work hard to keep it. When times are good, workers tend to take their jobs for granted and complacency becomes the norm. For the responsible worker, however, the economic climate does not determine his attitude and effort.

Considering a Command

In his letter to the church at Colosse, the apostle Paul directly addresses the issue of our work: "Whatever you do, work at it with all your heart, as working for the Lord, not for men" (3:23).

I know, I know. That was one of your favorite Bible quotations until I applied it to your job. But by reading this command in its context, we see that Paul intended it to be understood in light of your 9:00 to 5:00 routine.

> Slaves, obey your earthly masters in everything; and do it, not only when their eye is on you and to win their favor, but with sincerity of heart and reverence for the Lord. Whatever you do, work at it with all your heart, as working for the Lord, not for men, since you know that you will receive an inheritance from the Lord as a reward. It is the Lord Christ you are serving. (Colossians 3:22-24)

Notice the phrase "work at it with all your heart." An attitude that says, "Ho hum, when I get around to it, another day, another dollar," is not allowed. Rather, Paul commands that a "give it all you've got, nose to the grindstone" mentality should permeate our every activity. As one commentator pointed out in reflection on this passage, "If more Christian employees today served their employers with genuine concern and as though they were serving God, quality and productivity would increase dramatically!"[2]

From this direct biblical command we can draw two specific principles of application.

First, whatever the specific task before us, our work is to be done for God's glory rather than our own satisfaction. We develop negative attitudes because we feel cheated out of the fulfillment that is rightfully ours. But when we take our focus off of ourselves and place it where it belongs, the issue of how we perform our duties becomes far more significant than what duties we perform.

Second, since any job we perform is to God's glory, it should be done in a first-rate manner. Striving for excellence in all that we do is a biblically based responsibility, not just some motivational terminology from professional improvement seminars. How can we expect to glorify God with less than our best effort?

When we fall into a victimization mentality in relation to our jobs, we rob ourselves of the joys and rewards associated with viewing our work from God's perspective. He doesn't care *what* we are doing, He cares *how* we do it.

HEADING UPSTREAM

All of us want to be happy in our jobs, but few of us are able to overcome the natural drift into complacency and irresponsibility. This is primarily due to a lack of intentional effort on our part. Professional excellence and fulfillment do not happen by accident. They come only when we develop certain habits in our professional lives. Whether you are an accountant, a welder, or a manager, adopting the following habits can help move you beyond mediocrity on the job.

HABIT #1: HOLD YOURSELF ACCOUNTABLE

You are responsible for your own job satisfaction—not your boss, not your salary, not your situation. Until you are willing to hold yourself accountable for your own attitude, you will be unable to rise above the negativism that so easily invades the workplace.

HABIT #2: WORK WITH PURPOSE

If your life objective is to bring glory to God through full use of the abilities He has given you, then it is only fitting that a sense of purpose permeate your work. Too often we detach our life objective from the daily grind.

We typically tie our degree of effort on the job to personal reward. If we anticipate the possibility of a raise or promotion, we work harder. Work motivation has been a primary factor in the success of free-market societies throughout history. However, when your effort is tied to the larger purpose of glorifying God, lack of immediate reward will not de-motivate you. When doing your best is an expression of worship to the Lord, consistent effort is a natural outgrowth. Typically, when an employee adopts this perspective, the personal rewards eventually follow.

HABIT #3: PURSUE SPECIFIC GOALS

Defining and pursuing specific goals has more immediate application on the job than in any other area of life. Those who settle for the status quo and seek to reach only the minimum requirements are least likely to advance. But those who stretch themselves to learn more in an effort to become better employees will find themselves being given more responsibility.

If you are in sales, make it your goal to expand your customer base by 25 percent in the coming year. If you are in manufacturing, seek to produce the highest quality product possible according to the expectations of management. If you are in management, try creative measures to improve staff morale and efficiency. Whatever your specific role, make the job interesting and rewarding by reaching for something new. Who knows, you may even find yourself looking forward to work!

HABIT #4: SEEK TO SERVE

Jesus taught an important principle that might be considered a hindrance to corporate advancement: "Whoever wants to become great among you must be your servant, and whoever wants to be first must be your slave—just as the Son of Man did not come to be served, but to serve, and to give his life as a ransom for many" (Matthew 20:26-28).

How can we expect to climb the corporate ladder if we act like a slave? Are Christians supposed to avoid all leadership roles in order to fulfill Jesus' mandate?

Actually, having a servant's heart is a key to success, especially in the business world. If you stop to think about it for a moment, it becomes clear. If you are an employee, the most important thing you can do is seek to make your boss a success. If you are the boss, your role is to make those under you successful. When you do that, your superiors see you as an asset and your subordinates see you as a friend.

In contrast to the conventional wisdom, it is better to push those above you to move further up the ladder and pull those below you up as you go. When we try climbing over the people ahead of us and kicking those below us, we make it virtually impossible to get up the ladder ourselves.

In short, it is best to serve others by trying to make them successful, rather than seeking your own advancement.

HABIT #5: WORK HARD

In recent years, there have been reports of an epidemic spreading throughout the Western work force: "workaholism." In order to avoid contracting this awful ailment, many have made a conscious effort to practice several preventative measures.

1. Never agree to work more than eight hours in a day.
2. Always take frequent and long breaks, regardless of deadlines.
3. No matter what, do not allow work to interfere with your social life.

Through strict observance of these rules, many have avoided the awful stigma associated with workaholism. Unfortunately, they have also avoided the rewards associated with hard work.

Don't get me wrong. I strongly agree that being addicted to work is a serious problem for some. Those who work unnecessarily long hours and neglect their family, church, and friends for their job are professionally irresponsible. But so are those who use someone else's excess to justify their own laziness.

There is no reason to be afraid of hard work. In fact, discipline and self-sacrifice are some of the most important qualities you can develop on the job. A sense of satisfaction and self-respect come over you when you know you've given your best effort to a task.

The book of Proverbs makes some strong statements about diligence on the job.

> Lazy hands make a man poor, but diligent hands bring wealth. He who gathers crops in summer is a wise son, but he who sleeps during harvest is a disgraceful son. (Proverbs 10:4-5)
> The sluggard craves and gets nothing, but the desires of the diligent are fully satisfied. (Proverbs 13:4)

It is important to keep work in balance with the other responsibilities of life. But during the time you have dedicated to the job, make sure you work hard—rather than hardly work!

SUCCESS

Mary was recently promoted to middle management and placed in charge of an important research operation within her company. Only in her late twenties, Mary is considered too young for such a responsible position by many of her coworkers. But Mary's competent and confident approach to her new assignment is quite impressive. Her ability to deal with people effectively, coupled with a willingness to go the extra mile, has made her a valuable asset to the corporation.

From all appearances, Mary has it together in her professional life. But things were not always so good. In fact, Mary was at one time considered a problem employee within her company. Just a few years earlier, complacency and indifference characterized her professional reputation. Rather than dedicating herself to the task at hand, Mary focused her attention on what she disliked about the job. The current of negativism hampered her professional growth and pulled her further away from reaching her potential.

On one occasion, Mary seriously considered leaving her company in favor of one that would recognize and use her gifts. Fed up with her lack of opportunity and appreciation, she nearly jumped ship. But instead, she began to examine her own motives. Mary came to realize that what she needed was not a better job, but a better attitude.

It was a significant turning point in Mary's career when she began holding herself accountable for her perspective toward work. Rather than expecting the boss to give her a better assignment, she decided to stretch herself in her present role. Instead of passively waiting for a pay increase or promotion before going the extra mile, she voluntarily stepped in to serve where needed. She even expressed a willingness to accept certain tasks she had long avoided. No longer trapped in the bondage of negativism, Mary was free to become one of the most pleasant and productive members of the staff. It wasn't long before her diligence translated into more opportunities for growth, eventually leading to her promotion.

The most notable change in Mary is not her new office, her new title, or even her new assignment. Far more significant is her new attitude. It reflects a focused objective, a servant's heart, and a leader's maturity. In the context of professional responsibility, Mary would be a success story whether or not she ever received a promotion.

Bottom Line

There is a prevailing negativism in our society in the workplace. Emphasizing professional satisfaction over professional responsibility prevents us from finding meaningful purpose in our work. As a result, we rob ourselves of the joys and rewards associated with viewing work as a means to glorify God.

14
Financial Responsibility

Put not your trust in money,
but put your money in trust.
Oliver Wendell Holmes

Shortly after becoming engaged to the woman who is now my wife, a fear struck my generally daring heart. I was not afraid of commitment or the other common sources of cold feet prior to a wedding. I knew that I had found the most wonderful woman in the world, and I was happy that she was willing to settle for a mediocre guy like myself. The reason for my concern was money. We didn't have much of it. More significant, however, was the fact that I knew nothing about how to handle the little we had.

Perhaps my fear was motivated by the knowledge that a leading source of marital disharmony is financial pressure. I'd seen many couples worrying and arguing over how and where to spend the money. She wants a new dress, he wants a new car, and the collection agency wants to be paid. I determined prior to marriage that, to the extent possible, I would not allow financial issues to create a strain on our marriage. As a result, both my wife and I began the process of learning how to manage our finances.

Regardless of your economic level, you are responsible for the money God has allowed you to possess. Careful stewardship and wise financial decisions are required of everyone, not just the wealthy. As my wife and I learned during the early days of marriage, you don't need to have much money in order to learn how to use it properly.

DOWNSTREAM

Unfortunately, most individuals put little thought into how they handle their monetary affairs. Despite all that has been said and written about handling money, relatively few Christians take admonitions for good stewardship seriously enough to actually control and plan their finances. Yet how we handle our money is one of the most practical ways we impact our world, either for good or for bad.

CREDIT TRAP

Shawn and Alex Smith discovered early in their marriage the wonderful world of credit. As recent college graduates with money to spare, they were receiving pre-approved credit cards in the mail. "Imagine it," they mused, "getting several major credit cards from local banks without our even asking. How wonderful!"

Wonderful indeed. They were immediately able to purchase furniture for their bare apartment, kitchen supplies for their vacant cabinets, and clothes for their empty closet. Within a few weeks they had as much stuff as their parents had accumulated in decades. And it was all so painless. All that they had to do was walk up to the cashier and hand him one of those magic plastic cards.

Shawn and Alex were a bit concerned when the first set of credit card bills arrived. The total due was far beyond what they had expected. They never thought the purchases would add up so quickly. There was no way to pay the exorbitant bills with their meager incomes.

Fortunately, they located a line that read "minimum payment required" in the bottom corner of each bill. All anxiety ceased. After adding up the total minimum payments, they had plenty of money to cover themselves. Not only could they handle the bills this month, but they could go out and purchase a few final things with the unused portion of their credit allotment. Since it was made so easy by the credit companies, Buy Now, Pay Later became the slogan of the Smith family.

As time passed, Shawn and Alex found the cycle of debt becoming more difficult to handle. The combined minimum payments increased and became a major portion of their monthly expenses. They also noticed that, despite several regular payments, their total debt continued to increase. By making the "minimum required payment" on each credit card bill, they were not even covering the interest, let alone decreasing the principal. The wonderful world of credit seemed less wonderful all the time.

Eventually, Shawn and Alex found it necessary to consolidate their various debts into a single loan in order to handle the monthly payments. Due to the financial strain they had been experiencing, however, they were unable to set aside money for emergencies. So when the car broke down unexpectedly, they had to use a credit card to pay for the repair. That started the cycle again, and the debt increased even further due to several more "minor" purchases.

Today, Shawn and Alex are burdened with thousands of dollars of debt with no idea how they will pay it off. The stress has strained their relationship. It once seemed nice to have stuff without waiting. Now they both wish they'd never seen those dangerous plastic cards.

SPARE A DIME?

Kevin earns a very good living. He has always worked hard at the office and has received several promotions over the past few years. He and his wife, Shirley, recently moved into their "dream home" in a nice section of town. Although they are still fairly young, they have reached an admirable status by most standards.

Despite their general success, however, Kevin and Shirley find it difficult to financially support their church or other charitable organizations. They have found that their expenses have increased as rapidly as their income. As a result, there seems to be less extra money to give away than ever before.

Kevin has often found himself embarrassed when asked for contributions to help the homeless or some other worthy effort. He has enough money to live in a lovely house, drive a nice car, wear designer clothes, and take exotic vacations every year, but not enough to help the less fortunate. At one time he felt bad about it. Now he becomes angry at the pastor and others who make him feel guilty by talking about giving. *After all,* he thinks, *I work hard for a living, and it is none of their business what I do with my money!*

It's not that Kevin wouldn't like to give. He envies those who are wealthy enough to give large sums of money to the church. He has often said that he would be willing to finance an entire mission project if he had the means. Kevin would sacrifice thousands if he were richer. At present, however, he can't even spare a dime.

POOR RICHARD

Richard and his wife live in a small, one-bedroom apartment furnished with old, worn-out furniture. They have no money saved, drive a broken-down car, and find themselves barely surviving from check to check. In short, they live at the national poverty line.

Such financial struggling is to be expected of a newly married couple just starting their life together. After all, sacrifice in the early days is part of marriage. However, Richard and his wife are not newlyweds. In fact, they recently celebrated their forty-fifth wedding anniversary. Richard is nearly sixty-eight years old and has less money today than when he was eighteen years old. The check on which they so heavily depend is not a paycheck but a Social Security check. It is, at this point, their only source of income.

In his younger years, Richard earned a pretty good living. His factory job paid a higher than average wage, enabling him to raise his children in a comfortable home with nice clothes and plenty to eat. They paid their taxes and bills without fail and even gave a tenth to the church on a regular basis. They were by no means rich, but they did just fine.

What happened? How did Richard end up with so little after earning a good living for so long? Like so many others, Richard never considered saving a priority. He did not understand the value of putting a few dollars aside when they were more useful in the present. Although the cumulative income from his more than forty years of work would be quite impressive, none of it was reserved for a rainy day. Now, as a result of his negligence, Richard is without an umbrella.

LEAN PURSES

In 1926, a man named George Clason began publishing a series of pamphlets designed to teach wise handling of money.

Using parables set in the culture of ancient Babylon, he developed several timeless principles of financial stewardship. More recently, this series has been compiled into a single volume titled *The Richest Man in Babylon.*

Throughout this series of parables, the reader is privileged to eavesdrop on the wise instruction of a man named Arkad. Arkad is, as the title indicates, the richest man in all of Babylon. He has earned his vast wealth by consistently applying several principles of financial stewardship. Due to his success, men from throughout the East come to him for instruction on how to acquire gold. Those willing to heed his advice reap the benefits of financial success.

On one occasion, Arkad advises his students to save a tenth of their income, regardless of the amount. Many of them considered that unrealistic due to their economic status. In response, Arkad shares some insightful thoughts.

> "Some of your members, my students, have asked me this: 'How can a man keep one-tenth of all he earns in his purse when all the coins he earns are not enough for his necessary expenses?'" So did Arkad address his students upon the second day.
> "Yesterday how many of thee carried lean purses?"
> "All of us," answered the class.
> "Yet, thou do not all earn the same. Some earn much more than others. Some have much larger families to support. Yet, all purses were equally lean. Now I will tell thee an unusual truth about men and sons of men. It is this: That what each of us calls our 'necessary expenses' will always grow to equal our incomes unless we protest to the contrary."[1]

Arkad's wisdom applies just as directly to our generation as it did to his ancient students. No matter how much money we make, we will always come up with reasons we cannot apply principles of wise financial handling. Our "lean purses" prevent us from giving or saving and often prompt us to borrow beyond our capacity to repay. But as with Arkad's students, we all earn different incomes and have different levels of responsibility. Why, then, do we all have the same problems? It is because we do not, as Arkad suggests, "protest to the contrary."

HEADING UPSTREAM

If you are like me, tracking the Dow industrial average and reading the *Wall Street Journal* may be beyond your level of financial expertise. Perhaps balancing the checkbook is the most intense fiscal challenge you face on a monthly basis. Don't feel bad. Financial responsibility does not require an MBA degree or blue chip stocks. Even if you have little income and no understanding of the world economic climate, you are completely qualified to begin moving upstream on the river of personal finance.

If you were to set out on a quest to compile the most commonly espoused advice on financial management, you may be surprised at just how brief your summary report would be. Read all the books, articles, and pamphlets you can find, and the general conclusions will be the same. There are only a handful of principles that will set you on the path toward financial responsibility. These principles are the same for everyone, regardless of economic level. The dollar amount is not important. Consistency in application is the real key to success.

PRINCIPLE #1: SPEND LESS THAN YOU EARN

Live within your income. It sounds simple, doesn't it? Yet for millions of people in this country it is not a reality. In fact, many see it as a virtual impossibility, not because of their low income level but because of their high lifestyle expectations. Our entire economy is driven by the debt machine, and it traps the unsuspecting.

There is nothing new about credit. It is an economic system that has been around since the beginning of time. But it has never been as all-consuming as it has become in the Western world in the past several decades. Almost no one pays cash for anything these days. If the money is not available, saving until we can afford to buy doesn't even enter our minds. Simply charge it, and take it home today. Unfortunately, as with Shawn and Alex, the ease and convenience of credit can quickly transform into the stress and bondage of financial overextension.

The average working person has to make some sacrifices in life. The sooner we are willing to go without, the shorter the period of sacrifice will be. On the other hand, those who are unwilling to sacrifice in the early days will be forced to do so later. And when that period of sacrifice comes, it will be much longer and more difficult to accept.

My wife and I started our life together nearly two thousand dollars in debt. With little income and another year of college to finance, that debt seemed quite staggering. Yet, we determined that our first financial goal would be to pay it off as soon as possible. We had no idea when we made that commitment just how much sacrifice it would require. While our other newly married friends were furnishing their apartments and driving new cars, we dined on a folding card table and car-pooled to work. As difficult as those years of sacrifice were, however, they enabled us to get ahead of the credit game and begin living on cash.

By way of contrast, those who were unwilling to live within their means during the early days of marriage now find themselves confronted with a large dowry of debt that must be paid. Whereas our period of sacrifice serves as a nostalgic reminder of when we did without, theirs serves as a bitter aftertaste to former luxuries.

God has entrusted each of us with a certain income level. It is our responsibility to live within our means. Although there are some good reasons to use credit, they are rare. In general, it is wise to avoid debt at all costs by spending less than you earn. The long-range dividends are well worth the sacrifice.

PRINCIPLE #2: GIVE SOME

Have you ever noticed that the people who complain when the pastor raises the issue of money are usually those who never give a dime? Those who make giving a consistent habit understand its value and are free to be generous. Those who protect their wallets at all costs end up paying the biggest price.

Giving away a portion of your income as an expression of gratitude to God is a vital step toward gaining proper financial perspective. It serves as a reminder that He owns it all and that the true source of provision is the Lord. Failure to understand this fundamental concept is one of the primary reasons so many Christians worry about money. After all, with God out of the picture, our up-and-down economy can strike fear in the heart of anyone trying to make it alone.

Giving is not, as many teach, compulsory. I have been in churches where the pastor used fear tactics to motivate members to give. "If you don't give willingly, the Lord may have to send you to the hospital to have your tithes taken out." Such statements present God as a crooked loan shark who'll break your legs if you can't pay up. I have actually heard church members connect flat tires and engine problems with a late tithe payment! I believe strongly in regular giving to the local church. However, I give out of gratitude and love for God, not because I fear divine retribution.

Yes, giving is a responsibility. But it is also a privilege. When you place that check in the offering plate or send it to a charitable organization, you are making two statements. The first is one of thanks to God for His provision. The second statement is one of trust. You are confirming that the Lord owns everything and that there is no need to worry, because He will care for your needs.

> So do not worry, saying, "What shall we eat?" or "What shall we drink?" or "What shall we wear?" For the pagans run after all these things, and your heavenly Father knows that you need them. But seek first his kingdom and his righteousness, and all these things will be given to you as well. (Matthew 6:31-33)

PRINCIPLE #3: SAVE SOME

For a number of years I neglected this important principle of financial stewardship. There always seemed to be more immediate uses for the money than to let it sit in a savings account. After a while, however, I realized that there was never going to be a perfect time to start saving. Once one financial hurdle was crossed, another came. The ideal timing never arrived. So despite our bills, debts, and desires, we started putting a grand total of $25 per paycheck into a savings account. Today, we are worth well over $2 million! Not really. But we did begin an important habit, which is certain to reap long-range benefits.

It has been estimated that the average American saves less than 5 percent of his total income. We are one of the richest nations on earth, yet we cannot find a way to save a nickel out of each dollar we earn. As a result, only 2 percent of Americans reach age sixty-five financially independent. And when it comes to leaving something for the next generation, you can forget it. Yet the Bible clearly admonishes us to consider such long-range financial matters.

> Go to the ant, you sluggard; consider its ways and be wise! It has no commander, no overseer or ruler, yet it stores its provisions in summer and gathers its food at harvest. (Proverbs 6:6-8)
> A good man leaves an inheritance for his children's children. (Proverbs 13:22*a*)

You do not need to understand no-load mutual funds or high-yield certificates of deposit to start setting money aside each month. When you reach the point of retirement planning, you can seek the advice of professionals. Don't allow your limited knowledge of the financial world to keep you from taking the first step. Start by setting a budget that includes a designation for savings. Again, the amount is not as important as beginning the habit. The long-range accumulation will take care of itself.

IMPACT

In the effort to impact our world for good, Christians should attempt to be part of the solution, rather than part of the problem. Indebtedness, lack of long-range planning, and the inability to give all contribute to the overall financial malaise of our culture. When we begin acting responsibly with our finances, who knows how God will use us in the long-run?

Around the turn of the century, the founders of the Union Oil Company, Lyman and Milton Stewart, had a great impact upon their own and future generations by investing their wealth in the propagation of Christian ideals. They founded the Union Rescue Mission to help those in need, an institute of higher learning later called Biola University, and a local church with a worldwide missions outreach, the now historic Church of the Open Door. More than one hundred years later all three of these institutions continue to meet needs, train future leaders, and spread the Christian message.

During an era of almost exclusively liberal theological persuasion, the Stewarts also funded a much needed series of articles by leading scholars of the time on foundational issues of Christian truth. Those articles became known as "The Fundamentals" and gave rise to much of the evangelical scholarship we now take for granted.

A century later, millions of people benefit from the investment made by these godly gentlemen. I personally had some level of involvement with each of the institutions established through the Stewarts' financial backing. I attended seminary at Biola University, supported the homeless through the Union Rescue Mission, and had the opportunity to grow and serve in the Church of the Open Door for several years. I am one of many who are thankful for the ways in which God has blessed the financial impact of the Stewarts upon their world.

Although few of us will ever reach the level of impact of Lyman and Milton Stewart, we can still become part of the solution to this world's ills. By applying the principles of financial responsibility in our lives, God can use our faithfulness in ways we may never realize.

SUCCESS

Stan grew up in a well-to-do family in the affluent part of town. His father was a successful businessman who worked long and hard to give his family the very best. As a result, Stan never learned how to do without. He entered adulthood expecting to maintain the level of comfort and luxury to which he had grown accustomed. Unfortunately, his father was no longer around to foot the bill.

When Stan left home he had an excellent job with a pretty good income. He had obviously inherited his father's savvy business mind and did well in his career. But the more money that came in, the more Stan spent. He saw no reason to wait for a nice car, comfortable furniture, stereo system, or any of the other things he was used to having. As a newly married guy with a good income, everyone in the world was willing and eager to give him a line of credit. Why not take advantage of their generosity?

It wasn't long before Stan's monthly bills surpassed his monthly income. Even keeping up with the various "minimum monthly payments" became difficult. Then, without warning, Stan encountered some severe health problems. After a brief hospital stay, the doctor cautioned him to slow down in his professional career. His body could not take the physical drain his long hours were placing upon it any longer. With more bills from his doctors and the hospital, Stan found his income lowered due to a scaled back career.

Due to a combination of irresponsible spending patterns and unexpected health problems, Stan faced thousands of dollars of debt with a limited capacity to repay. Others counseled him to walk away from the debts by claiming bankruptcy, a perfectly legal way to avoid the consequences of his actions. "After all," they said, "it isn't your fault that you had health problems." But as a Christian, Stan believed that it was his responsibility before God to repay all of his debts. So he took the first step on the long road of repaying his creditors.

The first thing Stan and his wife did was begin giving, a habit they had neglected. Their second step was to begin budgeting, enabling them to spend with a plan. As a result, their money matters had a focused purpose. They started living within their means and put all extra money toward repaying their debts. It has not been easy. In fact, after years of discipline and second-hand goods, they are still paying off the last of their creditors. But the rewards associated with fulfilling their financial plan and the freedom from debt have far outweighed the temporary burden of making sacrifices.

Stan has taken the lessons he learned from his own financial mistakes and has started helping others who find themselves with little income and many bills. As one in the midst of his journey out of the credit trap, he knows how hard it can be to apply the principles of financial responsibility. But he also knows how rewarding it can be to move upstream against the tide of a culture consumed by the importance of possessions.

Stan and his wife do not own a house, drive a new car, or live in the lap of luxury. Nor will they likely leave a legacy such as Lyman and Milton Stewart. But they are successful nonetheless. They are freeing themselves from the debt trap, they are giving to the needy, and they are well on their way to reaping the long-range benefits of financial responsibility.

BOTTOM LINE

Regardless of your economic level, you are responsible for the money God has allowed you to possess. Careful stewardship and wise financial handling are required of everyone, not just the wealthy. Even if you have little income and no understanding of the world economic climate, you are completely qualified to begin moving upstream on the river of personal finance.

Several simple principles will set you on the path toward financial responsibility. First, spend less than you earn. Second, give some. Third, save some.

Conclusion

How does one address the issue of personal responsibility without seeming insensitive to the painful realities of life? As I said at the beginning of this book, life is not easy. It has not been my intention to suggest otherwise. Yet it is adversity in life that compels us to seek a balanced view of responsible living.

On one extreme are those who deny the strength of life's current, making themselves victims by default. You cannot overcome obstacles that you refuse to acknowledge. On the other extreme are those who acknowledge the current but see it as an irresistible force. Because they perceive themselves as helpless victims of its pull, the river of life carries them downstream.

In order to overcome life's obstacles, we must maintain a balanced perspective of adversity. Yes, life is difficult. But we do not have to remain victims of its downward pull. We can pick up the paddle of responsible living, face the current, and begin actively going against the flow. As someone has said, the difference between stumbling blocks and stepping-stones is the way a man uses them.

Taking personal responsibility for the direction of our lives includes consistent commitment to several important principles. First, we must develop a life map that is consistent with reality. Doing so requires a willingness to discover, accept, and live the truth, regardless of how difficult or unpleasant it may be.

Second, we must take personal responsibility for our own choices and their consequences, realizing that the law of sowing and reaping is as real as the law of gravity. When we make wise decisions, we reap positive results. When we choose the way of the fool, we reap folly.

Third, we must develop specific goals in life that enable us to achieve our overriding purpose of bringing glory to God. He has created us with tremendous gifts and abilities and holds us accountable for using them to their fullest.

When these principles are consistently applied, they serve as a steady source of resistance to life's natural downstream drift. The earlier they become a part of our lives, the more likely we are to advance toward successful living. As we move further upstream, the water becomes more calm and the resistance less strenuous.

But what about those who are so far downstream that advancement seems hopeless? What can be done when, despite their best effort, it is impossible to escape the river's pull? Is there ever a time when the obstacles are too big for a single individual to manage?

Certainly some individuals drift so far downstream that they become overwhelmed by the rapids of adversity. For that reason, it is important that the principles of personal responsibility be applied long before reaching the point of upheaval. Those who fail to do so often place themselves in need of crisis intervention from someone further upstream.

In general, however, responsible living enables us to overcome the obstacles of life. It keeps us out of those situations which create turmoil. It provides us with the means for reaching our objectives. And it sets us on a course that brings honor to God.

I began this book by expressing my deep desire to provide my son with the tools necessary to successfully overcome the obstacles of life. He will either become a victim of the difficulties ahead of him, or he will rise above them. My prayer is that his dad may begin setting the example of what it means to live a responsible lifestyle.

Notes

Chapter 1: Downstream Drift

1. M. Scott Peck, *The Road Less Traveled* (New York: Simon & Schuster, 1978), p. 15.

Chapter 3: Responsible Living

1. Jesse Birnbaum, "Crybabies: Eternal Victims," *Time*, August 12, 1991, p. 17.

Chapter 4: Wisdom Living

1. C. S. Lewis, *Mere Christianity* (New York: Macmillan, 1952), p. 54.

Chapter 6: The Necessity of Truth

1. Allan Bloom, *The Closing of the American Mind* (New York: Simon & Schuster, 1987), pp. 25-26.

Chapter 7: The Impact of Choices

1. Shelby Steele, "Affirmative Action: The High Price of Preference," *Los Angeles Times*, September 30, 1990, p. M5.
2. William Glasser, *Reality Therapy* (New York: Harper & Row, 1965), pp. 30-32.
3. Ibid., pp. 70-71, 110-11.

Chapter 8: The Benefits of Purpose

1. Ari Kiev, *A Strategy for Daily Living* (New York: Macmillan, 1973), pp. 2-5.

Chapter 10: Spiritual Responsibility

1. Steve Arterburn and Jack Felton, *Toxic Faith* (Nashville: Thomas Nelson, 1991), pp. 31-32.
2. Philip Yancey, *Disappointment with God* (Grand Rapids: Zondervan, 1988), pp. 183-84.

Chapter 11: Relational Responsibility

1. James C. Dobson, *Love Must Be Tough* (Waco, Tex.: Word, 1983), p. 55.

Chapter 12: Moral Responsibility

1. Karl Menninger, *Whatever Became of Sin?* (New York: Hawthorn, 1973), pp. 188-89.

Chapter 13: Professional Responsibility

1. James Patterson and Peter Kim, *The Day America Told the Truth* (New York: Prentice-Hall, 1991), p. 155.
2. Norman L. Geisler, *Colossians,* The Bible Knowledge Commentary: New Testament (Wheaton, Ill.: Victor, 1983), p. 684.

Chapter 14: Financial Responsibility

1. George S. Clason, *The Richest Man in Babylon* (New York: Signet, 1988), pp. 28-29.

Moody Press, a ministry of the Moody Bible Institute,
is designed for education, evangelization, and edification.
If we may assist you in knowing more about Christ
and the Christian life, please write us without obligation:
Moody Press, c/o MLM, Chicago, Illinois 60610.